Stop Your Baby's
Crying

Also available in the NANNY KNOWS BEST series
Successful Potty Training
Easy Weaning & First Feeding
Coping with Temper Tantrums

Stop Your Baby's
Crying

Nanny Smith

with Nina Grunfeld

VERMILION
LONDON

First published in 1996

3 5 7 9 10 8 6 4 2

First published in the United Kingdom in 1996
by Vermilion, an imprint of Ebury Press,
Random House, 20 Vauxhall Bridge Road,
London SW1V 2SA

Random House Australia (Pty) Limited
20 Alfred Street, Milsons Point, Sydney
New South Wales 2061, Australia

Random House New Zealand Limited
18 Poland Road, Glenfield
Auckland 10, New Zealand

Random House South Africa (Pty) Limited
PO BOX 337, Bergvlei, South Africa

Random House UK Limited Reg. No. 954009

A CIP catalogue record for this book is available from t
he British Library.

ISBN: 0 09 180935 5

Printed and bound in Great Britain
by Mackays of Chatham plc, Kent

CONTENTS

Unless a specific child is being written about, through-out the book your baby is referred to as 'he', not because of any bias but to differentiate you, the mother or child carer, from your baby.

SPECIAL 'CRYING BABY' AUDIO CASSETTE OFFER

Nanny Smith has recorded a unique audio cassette featuring four of the cries you are most likely to hear. By listening to the cries carefully, Nanny helps you to recognise them, understand what they mean and how to deal with them.

We hear: a hungry cry
a really unhappy cry
a tense cry
a wakeful, unsettled cry

To order your copy, please send a cheque for £1.99 (including p&p), made payable to Syndale Limited, to the following address. Offer is available in the UK only:

Nanny Knows Best
Syndale Limited
Myrtle Cottage
Rye Road, Hawkhurst
Kent TN18 5DW

CHAPTER ONE

All Babies Cry

Fifty years ago crying was rather taken for granted. If your baby cried he was said to be 'airing his lungs' and you offered him a soothing syrup. There were babies that cried in the day and a neighbour might take the baby out so that the mother could get on, and there were babies that cried in the night and parents would have to walk the boards because some babies were 'a bit of a nuisance'. Today we know the baby isn't a 'nuisance', he is trying to tell you something.

Crying for help
I am convinced that a baby does not ever cry without reason. He doesn't think to himself 'Well, I'll do a bout of shouting – that'll annoy her'. Nature makes a baby cry if he needs help – if he is very hungry or in pain or very lonely. If a baby doesn't have a reason for crying then he doesn't cry. It is a fact that if you have a group of babies and one or two of them are crying, the others don't cry in order to copy them. You'd think they might cry because they were being disturbed but they're not. They don't notice the other babies' cries and they don't need anything so there is no need to cry.

For adults crying is usually a sign of great

unhappiness, but when a baby cries it's a signal that something is wrong. It doesn't necessarily mean that he is unhappy, more that he is angry, and is calling for help, although to a mother his shouts may sound accusatory 'Why aren't you looking after me properly?'

Do clever children cry most?

People often say about a crying baby 'He'll grow out of it – crying babies are the clever ones' in the belief that very active crying babies are very, very intelligent. Of course, occasionally they are, and very often they are not. Certainly it is true both that one baby cries more than another and that he will grow out of his constant crying, probably before the end of his first year. I suppose when your baby is crying during the night it is comforting to think that at least you are suffering for the sake of an intelligent child. I do think that crying children have different temperaments from placid children. They don't relax as easily, they are often wriggly, wriggly babies and later very alert, bright, sensitive people.

It is interesting that so often a child with a crying problem has parents, or at least one parent, who had the same problem. I've received many letters from mothers of crying babies, who were themselves also criers. So it may be that the baby who cries a great deal inherits this trait from one of the parents. A child inherits the same nose, legs and everything else as one or other of his parents, so why shouldn't he have the same personality? And even within families children's personalities vary. The first baby of a family I know was a joy, he never cried, the second baby screamed all night. All babies are different.

Of course babies are very influenced by their surroundings and by the person who cares for them in their day-to-day life, but on the whole if a baby is going to be a crying baby whatever you do he will still be a crying baby.

'Am I really a bad mother?'

Animals with young don't go to another animal's young to comfort them, they only go to their own - they know their cries and are connected as it were with an invisible thread. Human mothers may not feel confident of knowing their children's cries immediately, but they very often do. When I worked at a maternity home the mothers would know the cries of their babies even if they were in the next door room and very often a mother would say 'I heard Stephen having a good old shout' and she would be right, it *was* her baby who had been shouting. It's a form of telepathy, a mother can feel it, she knows it is her baby crying.

When a baby cries, his mother's initial reaction is to try and do something about it and it is sometimes so frustrating for her when whatever she does has no effect. So she is not only having to put up with the piercing noise and her own extreme tiredness, but also possibly the feeling that she has failed as a mother to understand what her baby needs. But she shouldn't feel a failure. She may well be doing the job of mothering to the best of her ability and still have a shouting baby no matter what she does. It is a fact that some babies cry and you simply cannot find the reasons why.

Is he annoying the neighbours?

When a baby is crying you wish with all your heart that he would stop because you feel so sorry for the little child but you may also feel anxious about disturbing the people next-door. Of course your baby probably can be heard by the neighbours sometimes, but not nearly as much as you imagine, because his link is with you and his cries affect you much more than anyone else. There may still be a worry, either because the neighbours are so friendly that you don't want to ruin their nights, or because they are so aggressive that they may bang on the wall because they can't bear the noise any longer.

That makes you more worried because your child cries even when he is in your arms. It's a stressful experience having a baby and your hormones are rampaging and haven't settled down so you really do feel hopeless, helpless and frustrated.

People do get very tired being responsible for a baby. Being tired they then get worried about things that they would not have worried about normally – everything gets on top of them and is magnified. You know yourself, even when you are tired after one late night – it is much, much worse if you've had a disturbed evening and a night which has been broken up into five little cat naps. Babies are relentlessly demanding, when they want you they want you no matter what time of day or night it is – anytime is the same for a baby if he's hungry or cold.

The tyrant in the cot

There doesn't seem to be any pattern or logic whatsoever to when babies cry so you can't seem to plan to fit in with the crying. Sometimes they cry a great deal in the night, and sometimes not at all, so you can't decide 'He's going to cry in the early morning so I'll go to bed early and then I can have some sleep before he wakes me up', because then he doesn't go to sleep until 3 a.m. when he suddenly drops off.

Anybody giving birth to a baby for the first time can really have no idea of the effect it will have on her life because this tiny person in a pretty cot is really and truly a tyrant who needs to be fed and cared for. Of course, if you have a baby that happens to be the kind that is fairly amenable then it is quite fun and although you are tired it is rather nice. However, when you get the next baby and he doesn't follow that pattern but shouts a lot and the first baby minds very much that this interloper has come into his life, this is very, very, often when mothers are at their wits' end. That in turn affects on the children, who start feeling worried about themselves and begin crying even more because the mother is anxious, so there isn't a relaxed atmosphere.

Double trouble

Quite often it is the second child who is the crier rather than the first. Although he may have a better deal because the mother isn't as fearful of him as she was of the first baby and therefore is more relaxed, the down side is that she also now has more to do. Added to this, the firstborn may dislike the newborn and become more demanding and so she has to deal with him as well which may make her short-tempered. The mother will thus be more tired and on a very short fuse. If she is not used to a crying baby, because the first was very amenable, she will be worried in case there is something really wrong with the new baby and even more worried in case she can't do anything about it.

Any baby brings along a sudden restriction of freedom which may be bitterly resented when a mother is very tired and just wants to sleep or do something for herself for a change. Suddenly she's on call all the time. A crying baby is even worse, because he also gets on a mother's nerves. In a way it is very disappointing that instead of being able to enjoy this dear little tiny person that really and truly belongs to you you find he turns out to be extremely trying. My heart goes out to people who have a 'six-to-tenner' – a colicky baby – because it just ruins all the fun of having a baby if your evening is completely wrecked. Even if a husband and wife take it in turns to hold the baby they can't sit and talk together.

Everyone gives different advice

People do give all manner of solutions to the problems of a crying baby and what helps one situation does not always help another. I wouldn't recommend following all the different advice people have given you – I would think it would be a great worry to the child because his life would be changing all the time whilst experiments were being carried out on him.

Trying out different advice is not going to calm him, it is likely to make him cry all the more. This is because babies and young children like life to be the same, every day. This is why I lay particular stress on the value for your baby, and indeed for yourself, of working out a routine. If your baby knows that every day is going to follow the same pattern it helps him settle down and you will benefit from doing certain things at certain times instead of always being rushed. Occasionally babies form their own routine which then you must always follow. If your baby never seems to want to do things at the time that your routine says to do them then make a note of your baby's timing and move your routine around to fit his.

Of course it is more difficult when there is an older child. If the first or other children are of school age then you have to fix a routine for the baby that fits in with taking them to school and looking after them. If the elder child is not yet at school then I would set the routine around the baby because with very careful planning the older child can fit in with what you have planned. When doing so many things like feeding a baby, either with the breast or bottle, you can put your arm round the older child and talk to him or read him a story or he can have a little game near you that he can do while you are occupied. The most common scenario is that they want to go to the loo the moment you start feeding the baby, so keep the pot under your chair. (See Chapters 2 and 7).

'My life is hell, days seem endless'

A baby or a small child crying continuously whatever you do does make you feel sad and worried and helpless and then resentful. And of course people have been led to do very aggressive things to the baby because whatever they do doesn't help, it doesn't make any difference and then they think 'After all I've done to help and he still doesn't stop' and throw the child on to the bed or violently shake him.

A mother who feels like doing this really must talk to someone about it, whether it is the health visitor or doctor. It will be a great relief to talk to somebody about it. You'll realise that you are not the only one who has a baby crying all night. Almost half of the babies I looked after cried in the night at some stage.

When it's time to walk away

When a tiny baby has cried a great deal and you have done absolutely everything possible to get him off to sleep and you know he isn't hungry, cold or hot, hasn't got any wind in his tummy and isn't ill, then you are quite justified in putting the baby down and tucking him in cosily and walking away, even if he is crying. You have done your very, very best and it is much better to walk out of the room – count to ten as it were – perhaps have a little drink and look at the paper. You know the baby cannot get out of his cot and can come to no harm, so you need very much to care for yourself rather than lose your temper with your child. It is a great safety valve to leave the crying baby where you can't hear him and gather your resources.

Better still, if this is possible, is if another person – a very kind, trusted friend or a grandmother or partner – can take over for a short time. It means the mother can relax because she knows the baby is being well cared for by someone else and she has time to wind down, even lie down or go out for a walk. I've heard of cases where an old school friend or other reliable person has moved in and the mother has been able to go out for a while, away from all the hassle. She can then relax and that reflects on the baby, he can relax too.

A baby's relationship with his mother can be a vicious circle – if the mother is becoming more and more anxious while trying to console her baby, this will reflect on the baby who too will become more and more anxious. Babies and children, like dogs, are very sensitive to atmosphere.

CHAPTER TWO

Four Golden Rules

IF YOUR BABY DOES CRY A LOT I WOULD REVIEW MY lifestyle; I think the chief thing to aim for is a peaceful day. For somebody who has a house and a husband or partner and possibly more than one child it is often quite difficult to do the best for each member of the family – if there are tensions in your family, for one reason or another, do try and sort them out or the tension will affect your baby. I always tried to think about the child and what was best for him, but then caring for children was my career and my life's work, whereas someone having her first baby has before her an untrodden path with confusing signposts in the form of conflicting advice.

These four golden rules are applicable to every child from a new baby up to a five year old. If you follow them they should help to make your baby's life more peaceful, and yourself more relaxed and in control.

*The first Golden Rule is about
trying to keep calm.*

✦ Your baby will thrive on peace and quiet

(and so will you).

During the day a new baby should be in a quiet corner where there isn't a lot going on. You don't have to tiptoe a lot and talk in whispers, but do put him in the next room, or even in his bedroom, so that he is away from all the hustle and bustle and can just relax and sleep. In those first few months a peaceful day helps to make for a peaceful night. Babies nowadays do seem to be so terribly over-stimulated during the day and then expected to be quiet at night-time. If you aim for a tranquil day the baby is going to sleep most of the time and when he wakes he is going to just look round and you can get on with your life in the household. Our babies were left outside in their prams all morning just watching the leaves, or inside if it was a cold day. Babies fall asleep anywhere and everywhere, if there is a peaceful atmosphere.

Give them a few quiet years

Even as they get older, babies and toddlers need a relatively quiet life – a few toys and a period of rest during the day and an outing to the park, or if this is not feasible, then taken out to do shopping, given a change of scene as it were. When my children were two we went out for tea, or had a little friend round for tea, once a week at most. There is the rest of one's life to socialise, but if a child can have a few peaceful years at home, meeting children of course, but not continually thrust into a busy atmosphere where there is a great deal of competition for popular toys, it will stand them in such good stead for later. You will benefit from a quiet life too.

Attend to his needs first

The important thing in the first few years of childcare is to give a great deal of your time to the child. I don't mean playing with him all the time, rather not trying to rush things with him because you've got to write to the bank manager. Of course, sometimes you have to do whatever you have to do but children can certainly sense that you want to get rid of them because you have something else to do and that only makes them more demanding. It is difficult in a busy life and if there are urgent things that you really must attend to then I think the only thing you can do is to write a list of what you have to do and then focus on the child and calm him down. When you have attended to the child's needs and he is settled you can get on. Sometimes it takes a very short time – as far as possible, keep calm.

If you can do the things you feel you simply must do while the child is having a rest or a sleep in the morning or afternoon then it is all for the best. Of course, the child cannot take over your life completely, but whether it is a baby or a toddler who is crying you must deal with his problems because you are the one who is responsible for him. What you must try and remember is that this bit of your life is only going to last for such a short time. Within a few years your child will be making far fewer demands.

Giving yourself breathing space

If children have always been left on their own (or with their brothers or sisters) to play and explore their toys they are much happier than if you have always joined in with them. It is their world. Of course occasionally you must play with them, throwing them balls in the park for instance, but if their routine is for them to play on their own then they are very happy to do so and it gives you a little freedom as well. I don't mean that you should never play with your child – if they are playing and they say 'You have a turn, Mummy' or 'You do it, Mummy', then of course you should join in, but otherwise if they can play on their own it so encourages their imagination. It also means they are not always crying for you to play with them. Every night I would get out two or three toys for the child to play with the next morning, preferably not the same as the day just over and I would start a play – I might build a little tower with a few building blocks or I might put out a biscuit and a little water in a tea pot, lay the table for a suggested tea party for teddy. Then they would find it in the morning and be so thrilled.

The second Golden Rule is about doing the same thing at the same time of day, so the baby knows what to expect.

✦ Be consistent; babies flourish on routine

(and it will help you too).

Whenever possible I have stuck to a routine with children (see My Tried and Tested Routines, Chapter 7). Children do so enjoy and benefit from a life of routine. This doesn't mean that you have to be hidebound and feel put out if the routine goes awry, but if you can more or less keep to it, you will find it is an enormous help.

From the very beginning it is really essential to establish a feeding routine, but of course until a baby gets established, which is by about six weeks, you can fit in with his demands providing you have no other demands on your time. If a baby is very hungry he must be fed on demand, but it is so much easier for you and the household if you know at what time the next feed is going to be needed. Even if a routine is difficult to get going, aim for it, it doesn't matter if at first it is not always a firm routine. By two months it will be a lot easier.

If you have more than one child you can still use a routine – you fit the older child in with the baby as explained in Chapter One. One of my toddlers used to sail her boats in her younger brother's bath; if you just give an older child enough attention he will happily fit in with his sibling – except in the case of school timetables which are inflexible.

Try to look ahead

Once you have a routine as far as the baby is concerned, that is what always happens. After three months he will recognise any routine that is introduced and expect it to go on for ever – he is already so much more aware of what is happening. So, at this stage you must try and imagine the future and whether you will want this or that part of your routine to carry on into the future as it will be difficult to stop (see the third Golden Rule below). One of the things that people do have problems with is taking the little baby into their bed when he cries or in order to feed him. This is one of the things to avoid doing, at least once the child is three months old. Before three months it really doesn't matter if the child is in your bed because he won't be so aware of where he is, he could be anywhere and it might be easier for you if he was in your bed. (See Chapters 3-6).

It is so difficult for a first time mother to know what routines she is going to regret having started or not having introduced. I would suggest that you trust your instincts. You and the baby have an affinity and you may well have a feeling about what makes him happy and comfortable.

If you don't have such a feeling and you really are at your wits' end and feeling insecure about having to care for this little person, you will, I am sure, have one close friend who has already had children – or a health visitor or a doctor or someone you really trust – whom you can talk it over with. Think very carefully about whom you trust and then stick to that.

Children do like consistency in all things. For instance, when you sit the child in his high chair and do up the safety straps, that is all part of the routine of sitting in a chair to eat. But if for one or two days you are in a hurry and omit to do up the straps he may say 'Strap, strap' because that is what he is used to, yet a few days later if you have time again and want to put his straps on, he may then refuse because he has now accepted another routine.

The Third Golden Rule is about introducing changes.

✦ Never make changes abruptly

(he'll accept them better if you go slow).

Changes of any kind in a child's life should be introduced slowly and cautiously – changes of food, lifestyle, routine or anything else. Food and bedtime are the two things in a routine which do sometimes get out of order. If you find your child's bedtime has become later and later because you are busy, or the child is involved with something and doesn't want to go to bed, and you want suddenly to get back to a proper hour it can take time. You will have to work his bedtime back very carefully and slowly, fifteen minutes every other day or your child will resist.

For a little baby the only change in his life should be

food because as long as he is little he will be put to bed at the same time. When you are changing from breast and bottle to cup, or milk to solids, you must take things very gradually. Try and imagine how your child is feeling with something different put in his mouth. I always started very slowly and quite often they were delighted with the new taste or experience and then it wasn't a problem, but it can be.

The fourth Golden Rule is about considering your child.

✦ Adopt the child's eye view: see what he wants and observe his needs.

You learn a great deal from a child's reaction to things. Sometimes through trying to see things through the child's eyes you get quite a different idea of how it might look to him. As far as possible you should try and do this. Children should always be treated with respect. I know babies are very happy in their mother's arms or grandma's arms, but they don't always enjoy being cuddled and passed round from person to person. They almost heave a sigh of relief when you put them down. If their tummies are full then they can't wait to be in their own cot. Some babies are very cuddly, but most are rather wriggly and would much rather be in their own space until they need you.

Find out what's wrong
Of course when a baby or a small child cries you must go to him and try and find out why he is upset. Sometimes you can find out what the trouble is and do something about it, sometimes you can't think what's wrong and don't know why he is making such a fuss.

When babies are very small it is fairly basic, it is usually because they are hungry or have a pain. (See A Quick Guide to What's Wrong, page 41). When children get to be two or three you can tell when they are over-tired or slightly unwell. When they start school sometimes there is someone in the class whom they don't get on with and it is a slight worry but usually you can really talk to a five year old, casually find out what it is that is making him sad, and help him sort it out.

Sometimes with children you think the problem is one thing and it isn't, it's another. You are doing your best and they push you away because you haven't understood them. I've seen parents trying to give their child more food when he is crying and rubbing his eyes, not because he is hungry but because he is tired. Very often, like adults when they are over-tired, what children would like to do best of all is go to bed. You put them into their cot or bed and they close their eyes and it is such a relief for them.

For 'naughty' read 'tired'

One evening I was staying with a friend, it was quite late and her little daughter was running around and being such a nuisance that her mother said 'If you don't behave I'll put you to bed!'. The little girl was only three or four and I could see she was dying to go to bed, but her mother hadn't noticed. Very often children are a nuisance when they are tired and they would just love to go to bed. Often children are threatened with bed, but it is not a punishment and shouldn't be looked upon as one. Children who are put to bed when they are beginning to feel sleepy will be perfectly happy, especially if it has been the same night after night.

CHAPTER THREE

When Your New Baby Cries

(0 – 3 Months)

WHEN A NEW BABY CRIES AND YOU ARE HIS mother, it is like animals with their young. Nature makes the mother try to do something about the cry and, of course, food in the form of milk does soothe the baby. He relaxes in his mother's arms and so she relaxes because she has been able to do something about the crying. However, each time a baby cries he isn't necessarily hungry, so you don't always have to pick him up and give him a feed or you will be exhausted. If you feel exhausted just leave him for five minutes. If you know you've done everything and he is still crying, there is nothing you can do, he's just having a little grumble. You should sit down and have a short rest yourself and try and switch off.

Work out your baby's problem

People say that you can 'spoil' a new baby if you pick him up. Well, how do you 'spoil' him, I would like to know? Babies are not calculating, they don't say to themselves 'I'll cry and then they'll pick me up'. If a baby did cry because he would like to be picked up, then he should be picked up because that is what he would like, but little babies don't do that. So the first thing is to work out what your baby's problem might be as only then can you take steps to solve it and make him happier.

Why Might Your Baby Cry Now?

There are babies who are criers. No matter what one does they still cry. Occasionally of course there is something wrong, but very often there isn't. Clearly a baby would not be making that noise for nothing but it is something that you just don't know about and so you can do very little about it. It may be that they just have a sad feeling.

A very new baby is almost always crying because he is hungry although he may cry because he is needing contact, in pain, restless, ill, unable to sleep or frightened in some way. His crying might also occur more at different times of the day or night, so when you are looking at the reasons for crying, below, look also at the different times of day he may be crying. It won't be long before you begin to understand what each of your baby's cries mean.

Crying and feeding

I would never leave a new baby to scream in order to try and condition him not to wake up in the night, although this hard hearted practice still persists. If a baby is hungry then he must be fed. I suppose a hungry baby would just scream and scream until he dropped off to sleep with exhaustion, but that is so unkind. He also wouldn't stay asleep for very long, the sleep would restore him and he would probably wake up and start crying again. Giving a baby a feed of milk doesn't take very long. I always fed babies between 10 and 11 p.m., but there was the thought that if you fed them much later, when they woke – maybe at 3 a.m. – they might then sleep until 8 a.m. rather than 6 a.m. as my babies did (see Chapter Seven).

Crying at the beginning of a feed

One of my children screamed at the beginning of her breast-feed. The doctor found out that she had laryngitis, so when she sucked it must have pulled painfully at her throat. The cause could also be thrush, when your baby would have a sort of white mould in his mouth – that might well hurt and you should consult the doctor.

Another cause is a blocked nose preventing him from sucking – if your nose is blocked you have to breathe through your mouth, but if you are sucking you can't do this. Ask your doctor about saline nose drops; or get a little cotton wool, dip it in olive oil so it is damp but not dripping. Twist it into a tiny piece so you can work just inside the baby's nostrils very carefully to remove anything that is stuck there. To help the baby you stroke the outside of the nose from the top downwards, working out the mucus, and then you can remove it with the cotton wool. If you are breast-feeding try and place the baby so that you are not squashing either of his nostrils. Make sure his mouth is still covering the entire areola.

If he is not getting his milk fast enough he might also cry. If you are feeding with a bottle you can see whether the milk is coming; certainly the baby will cry if the hole in the teat is very, very small and no matter how hard he sucks he doesn't get very much milk. It is the same with the breast – if the mother doesn't let down and there is no milk coming quickly he may get desperate too and begin screaming.

A baby might also cry at the beginning of his feed if his bottle of milk was too hot. Do check the temperature carefully before every feed. Always shake the bottle several times to make sure the temperature is even throughout before testing it.

Crying in the middle of a feed

Stopping a feed half way through to wind a baby is completely unnecessary and it can make a baby very unhappy to be interrupted in the middle of the feed. It is a very unkind thing to do. (See advice on winding, page 28.)

Crying at the end of a feed

You can tell if your baby is still hungry at the end of his feed. If he has not had enough to eat he will look a little bit unsettled and will try and find the bottle or breast and won't be as sleepy as he would be if he had a full tummy, but will look around and even cry. If that happened and I was bottle feeding, then I would give him a little more to drink and then at the next feed I would put more milk in the bottle. If you are breast-feeding, then I would just feed for another five minutes on top of your original ten minutes of each breast. It can be difficult for a breast-feeding mother to know if her child is really hungry or just wanting to suck for a little bit longer.

After the extra five minutes I would just gently take the breast away, cuddle him for a minute or two and then put him down. If he then carries on shouting it will mean he is hungry, so give him another five minutes. If you are worried that your baby is constantly hungry and that you do not have enough milk, although you probably do, you can always hire some scales and weigh him daily to reassure yourself that he is putting on weight.

Crying shortly after a feed

Quite often what happens is that you have filled up your baby's tummy and he has fallen asleep in your arms and so you've put him on your shoulder for a few minutes, for the wind to come up or down; then you have gently put him down, still fast asleep. If he woke up after a few minutes and started to cry I would suggest you go to him, pick him up and keep him rolled in his shawl, rest his head on your shoulder and cuddle him, walking him round the room. Alternatively, stand still and rock him gently – it is easier to rock a baby when you are standing up. If you have him in your arms you can see when his eyelids close and then you could put him very, very gently back down in the cot and put the cover over him, don't fuss tucking him in, and he will sleep. If he still doesn't sleep he might still be hungry and I would offer him more milk and go through the routine again. If it was night-time I would just leave the door open so enough light comes in for you to see what you are doing.

Sucking in his sleep

If a new baby cries between feeds, even half an hour after his last feed, it is because he has not had enough food and is hungry. I would feed him and then put him down (see Crying at the end of a feed, opposite). Another cause of crying half an hour after a feed is that the baby has fallen asleep in the middle of it. Sucking is quite an exhausting thing to do and sometimes babies do fall asleep before they have finished their feed. I always kept the feed in a jug of hot water and let the

baby sleep just for a few minutes, then I tested the
temperature of the milk again and just put the teat back
in his mouth; the baby would automatically suck. In my
experience babies very often suck when they appear to
be asleep. If the baby does tend to drop off to sleep
when being breast-fed, then let him sleep for a few
minutes and then try waking him so he can finish his
feed. This sounds easier than it sometimes is, so if he
won't wake up then I would put him down and be
prepared for him waking up half an hour later for the
rest of his feed.

Does he have a windy tummy?

When babies have wind there is a blueish tinge on the
top lip. He will also have a hard tummy. However, if
symptoms persist, it's advisable to see your doctor. In
babies a common cause of wind is air swallowed during
sucking; in a bottle-fed baby it may be that the hole in
the teat is too small. Wind is a problem for little babies,
so whenever I have finished feeding a baby I sit him
upright on my knee with one hand on his front and the
other on his back, leaning him slightly forward and
slightly to the left and almost stretch his little body
forward and the wind will soon go up or down. This
avoids all this curious banging on the baby's back which
I really think is so hard on the baby. Imagine having
your back banged after a meal. It seems to be a custom
which has been with us for a very long time.
Occasionally babies don't have wind, but people
assume they do.

Gently does it

A windy baby is very often made happier just by the
simple act of being picked up rather than lying on his
back – he is now upright in your arms and the wind can
come out more easily. If when you pick your baby up
his tummy is hard because he has wind, and if it doesn't

come out immediately I would put him on your shoulder, rub his back a little bit and then up or down would come the wind. I would then put him quietly back to bed again. Be very gentle about the whole thing and tuck him in. He has no reason to shout now but because he has been disturbed he might whimper a little bit and that can be ignored unless it gets louder. If it does get louder, then I would sit next to him and gently stroke his shoulders and forehead and cheeks and just talk very quietly to him, reassuring him with a calm voice. You know his tummy is filled and he is comfortable and he should sleep. If the stroking and kind words don't do any good and he is very upset and crying hysterically I would pick him up again and calm him down. (See Some Soothing Tips, page 48).

Is he upset by certain foods?

It can happen that when a baby is breast-fed and the mother has eaten, for example, beans and cauliflower and, strangely enough strawberries, it gives the baby tummy-ache. One of my mothers who was breastfeeding found that she had to avoid cauliflower and other 'windy' foods or the baby would have lots of wind and and would cry and cry.

If your baby is crying all day and all night you must seek help. One of the reasons may be that he is allergic to milk. If a baby can't tolerate dairy products he will probably swallow all his food and gain weight but he may scream all day and all night. I have known babies whose mothers have had to stop eating or drinking all dairy products whilst they were breast-feeding. If you suspect that your baby may be allergic, always consult your doctor as to what to do.

Crying and colic

If your baby cries once or twice in the entire evening it could be that he was over-stimulated, but a baby who screams desperately all evening, every evening, starting around sixish and finishing by 10 p.m. or 10.30 p.m. probably has what is known as 3-Month Colic. It can start with a baby of a few weeks old and can go on until he reaches three or four months. The minute you pick him up and hold him firmly upright he stops crying so you do know that is the best way to cope with it. However, there are times when there are things you really feel you must do and if this is the case then you must ask a friend or your husband to take over. It is very, very distressing and exhausting for the baby to be in such pain and to scream so much and very nerve-racking, frustrating and tiring for the people in charge. It is a very exhausting time in a new mother's life if her baby is crying and screaming all evening and then may sleep most of the night, but also may not.

What is colic?

Colic would seem to be something of a mystery; despite various theories it has not been established what causes it. What happens is that the baby screams and pulls his legs up, as though in unbearable pain but again, we do not know for sure whether he is in fact in pain.

It may be that colic is caused by something outside the baby – could it be his mother's tension and anxiety reflecting on him? Sometimes the problem almost seems to be almost inherited. I've had several letters from grand-parents telling me about their colicky daughters and now granddaughters. It did make me wonder if possibly the propensity of babies to suffer from colic is inherited.

How to help a colicky baby?

Once the baby is picked up and held upright against your shoulder very firmly, so his tummy is pressed against your chest, he stops crying. Until he outgrows the colic he will need to be picked up and held flat against you all evening. This is a great nuisance, but it won't last for long. Ignorant people will say 'Oh, he just wanted to be picked up.' Of course he did, by being held the pain is alleviated. The tiresome thing is that you are tired and you begin to wonder 'Will it ever end?' and of course it does. I think you just have to cope with it for those few months and wait until it passes. It is helpful if someone else takes turns with holding the baby.

If you simply cannot continue holding him because there is something you have to do and there isn't anyone to hand him to, then of course you must put the baby down – he will cry bitterly so I would close the door so you can't hear him, and then go back to him as soon as you've dealt with whatever it is.

In my day one nanny I knew had a baby who had colic so she filled a teat with cotton wool and kept it on the bottle so the baby could suck but wouldn't be sucking in air or food. Giving him this to suck did stop him crying, as I suppose a dummy might. This is worth trying. I did hear of someone giving a baby a sip of lemon juice, no more, and I was told that that helped with the colic tremendously. I don't know how this works and it's not to be recommended in every case, but this it might be worth trying.

Crying and sleeping

If a baby is hungry, then this may stop him both going to sleep and staying asleep, but it is not the only reason that a baby will have trouble sleeping. If it is not hunger, more often than not he will be restless because he is over-stimulated and will need gentle calming down. Often babies make a bit of a fuss when you put them down in the crib. They will usually soon drop off on their own, and so long as they aren't screaming you can always leave them for a few minutes, but they do find

31

it soothing if you gently stroke their foreheads for a minute or two, at the same time speaking to them in a calm, quiet voice (see Some Soothing Tips page 48).

Crying because unable to get to sleep

You know yourself you have friends who never shut up and you are exhausted by the end of the evening, but often over-tired and unable to sleep, whereas after a quiet evening you can go restfully to bed. After a party or gathering, Christmas or a christening babies and older children do have difficulty dropping off to sleep as the day has been so exciting. They are over-stimulated and wide awake. To get back to their normal sleep patterns they need peaceful, uneventful, predictable days in which to calm down and relax (See Chapter Two).

At an early age, up to three months, babies do usually fall asleep when they are tired, unless, of course, they are hungry or in pain. Nevertheless a baby does quite often find it difficult to settle if he has been passed around and jigged about by too many people. He becomes distressed and cries loudly. No doubt one could argue that if they always have noise and a lot of people around them they would get used to it, but I'm not sure that that is true.

Calming an exhausted baby

If I had a little baby who had had a very busy day and who I thought might be over-stimulated, I would pick him up and rock him in my arms very gently, standing up and talking quietly to him. It's a reassuring feeling for him to be very close to a familiar person, be it mother or nanny. I think it gives a feeling of security that the baby needs after a confusing day. I wouldn't necessarily give him another feed, it's comfort he needs. If babies are over-stimulated, they can't relax and then they cry. If you are a breast-feeding mother and pick up your over-stimulated baby he may well start searching for food. If so, there is nothing wrong with giving him a little suck, not because he's hungry, but because it is reassuring (See also Some Soothing Tips page 48).

Crying occasionally in the night

Only two of my babies slept through the night almost from birth, but it always seemed to me that if a baby was fed every three or four hours during the day then why shouldn't he be fed in the middle of the night? Why should he be expected to sleep from 10 p.m. to 6 a.m. without a feed? When my babies woke crying I fed them. If the baby is hungry it seems so mean to give him water. It does worry mothers that they will be forever waking in the night to feed a hungry baby, but in no time at all babies do stop waking in the night, usually at some stage between six weeks and three months. So around 2 a.m. or 3 a.m. you should expect to give your baby another feed and nappy change. Certainly some babies don't wake, but in my experience, most do.

Crying constantly in the night

If your baby sleeps badly and wakes all the time, this does not mean that he is hungry. I was up with one of my babies all the time, it was exhausting. All one can say is that there are adults who sleep very, very badly and wake every hour of the night, who have often been like that since they were children. The fact is that if you are a poor sleeper, you are a poor sleeper, and if you have a baby like this who yells in the night when you have looked forward to having him it is very depressing. There is no magic answer. Keep the atmosphere in his room as restful as possible and no bright lights. I think the best thing to do, however, if you have a small baby who is a poor sleeper, is to have him sleeping in your room. I always did until the child was a year old. It is so much easier for the mother or the nurse.

If your baby is very wakeful, all you can do is take him in your arms for a few minutes each time he wakes and then put him down again, (see also Some Soothing Tips page 48). You can't leave the baby to scream unless you are absolutely desperate in which case you might just have to leave him to shout. Of course you won't be able to for long for fear the noise might wake up the household and the neighbours.

Thumbs up for comfort

Sucking is very comforting for a baby and it is a blessing if he can find his thumb. If you are breast-feeding you might bring the baby in the bed with you and let him have a little suck until he falls asleep and then put him back in his cot. If you are exhausted he will obviously stay with you in your bed, but once he is over three months old it is best to take him back to his cot or it will eventually create the problem of returning him to his cot (see pages 19-20).

I was once asked what to do by a mother of a six-week-old son who cried most nights. She found it very wearing, especially after a Caesarian. She thought her child might have 3-Month Colic as nothing seemed to help.

I assured her that it was probably not colic as colic always happens in the evening and not at night. I told her that some babies do take time to settle into a routine. Some babies sleep much more than others, some sleep soundly most of the day and then they are awake at night.

I suggested that if her baby was restless he might be hungry and should be fed and she shouldn't worry that she was starting a habit that would never end as this was not the case. Little babies when they are hungry or in pain shout as their way of communicating; they must be reassured and hugged and given some milk and one must make sure that they don't have wind. I told her that she would soon find that a little reassurance helped, patting and stroking his forehead and talking to him quietly just for a while, picking him up quietly for just a short time and then putting him down very gently often stops the crying. A crying baby very often does want contact. I also advised her to try and lead as quiet a life as possible for the next few weeks to give them both time to settle into more of a routine.

Crying when waking
New babies do often cry immediately on waking up. It is instinct to cry when they wake because they want food then. On the whole, up to three months, babies wake every few hours and make a little bit of noise indicating that they need to be fed. It isn't as vociferous as when they are a little older.

Crying due to extreme temperatures
Extreme cold and heat would upset a new baby; if they do get very hot, for instance, they become fretful. Whenever I dress a baby I always imagine what I would wear that day if I was lying still and then I put the same amount of clothes on him. It's the same with covers – think how many covers you would want if you were lying next to him, unable to move.

Crying from being too hot
On a hot summer's day I would always put a baby in the shade, either under a canopy or, better still, under a tree because often the canopy is so small and may not

shade the baby completely when the sun moves. If it is very hot, babies are much better left indoors lying in a crib in a shady corner. Remember, they are lying quite still and not moving so you might even put a little jacket on them.

When I put the baby down, wherever it might be, but particularly out of doors, I check whether the sun is likely to shine on his face by lowering my head to the baby's level. A whimpering baby might well have the sun in his eyes and be trying to get away from it. I also look to see if there is something interesting for the baby to watch, such as a tree with the leaves stirring, rather than an expanse of sky and nothing else.

Getting into hot water
A whimpering baby might also be thirsty, especially in the summer. If it is a very, very hot day it is a good idea to give him a little drink of boiled water that has been cooled. I always keep a small jug of boiled water to hand, with a cover on the top so that dust cannot get in. Babies are quite happy to have a drink of water on a hot day. They only have sips which we give them with a spoon.

A baby might also cry from the heat of his bottle of milk or too hot bath water (see Crying at the beginning of a feed, page 25 and Crying at bathtime, page 38).

In his crib, I don't think that having too many covers on would make a baby cry, although he would get very fretful. However, make sure that he is not overwrapped as this could be very dangerous.

Never leave a child unattended in a parked car. Increasing heat in an enclosed space has proved fatal in a number of cases.

Crying from being too cold
It would have to be very cold to cause a baby to cry, if indeed the cold would make him cry at all. I remember babies pulling their mittens off in the park and they

would have purple hands they were so cold, but they never minded. However I have seen babies carried by their parents on a cold winter's day who are wearing snow suits – usually don't have mitts on and very often don't have a hat on either – or their snow suit hat has fallen down and they are crying and crying. I suppose they may be crying for another reason but they must have been frozen. They might also have got earache and then will cry in the night and their parents would have wondered why. One must always make allowances for the fact that whereas adults keep on the move out of doors, small babies are stationary, and to remember that since a lot of heat escapes from the head, babies with very litle or no hair simply must have a woolly bonnet on in cold weather.

Crying when worried

It is hard to tell for sure whether a baby cries because he is worried unless you can pin it down to a specific cause such as a loud noise (see page 38), a dog barking etc., etc.

Sharing her sorrow

However, if a mother is worried about what to do in a particular situation her own anxiety may be conveyed to the baby because of the very strong invisible attachment between them. Only she can tell whether there is something preying on her mind that could be transmitting her anxiety to her baby.

I think an incident that occurred when I was training certainly illustrates this. One of the babies in our care screamed continually night after night. This baby's mother was about 45, an elderly unmarried mother who had had a son when she was 20. She was now sharing a flat with her adult son and she did not want him to know that she had had this baby and so this baby was going to be adopted. His mother was very, very sad to let the baby go but she adored her grown-up son and nobody knew whether or not this little baby sensed how sad she was. She was in such turmoil, poor woman, she didn't want him to be adopted but it was the only way she knew how to cope with the situation. Perhaps her distress reflected on the baby.

Feeling unwanted

If you are tense and anxious it may be that your baby senses this and it is making him unhappy. And if at a subconscious level you are resenting the contraints and demands that he is imposing on you, he may be crying because he feels unwanted and insecure, particularly if you are holding or tucking him down too tightly or not closely enough to make him feel safe. When I wrap a baby in a shawl I always hold him quite firmly so he feels secure. On putting a baby of up to 3 months to bed I first roll him up in a shawl, keeping his arms down. On top of that I put a small sheet, and a blanket on top of that. I tuck him in quite firmly, having pulled the covers up over his shoulders before I tuck him in. I think babies like to feel secure – and they may be able to tell if someone is nervous about holding them. At bathtime for example, they need to be held securely – not too tightly, but not too loosely either.

Crying at bathtime

I wonder why some babies cry at bathtime? If the water was too hot or too cold a baby would protest, but they usually like their baths and enjoy being naked. I have always found that even if they were crying at other times they never cried in the bath. I always made sure the water was deep, not too hot or too cold and would hold the baby securely. I used very little soap so they were not too slippery and I lowered them into the bath and moved them about a little bit so that the water was going over their tummy. I never hurried a bath. Bathtime should be a time of enjoyment.

Disturbed by noise

Sounds like a door banging can startle babies. You can see them jump. If a baby was crying desperately then I would pick him up and reassure him but otherwise I would just say 'Ssshh, it's all right' and stroke his forehead, it would depend how distressed he was. Babies can be frightened by loud noises whether they are awake or asleep, and you must reassure them. When they have put a baby to bed, people very often talk in whispers and tiptoe round and turn the wireless down. It is much happier for the baby if everything carries on as normal so he can hear voices and the television. When all goes quiet the baby must think 'I'm alone, I'm out on a limb' whereas if he hears the daytime noises then he will think everything goes on as usual.

If you feel you really must vacuum just as the baby has gone to sleep, then go ahead – I don't think the baby will mind. When babies are tired they will sleep no matter what is going on, more or less. Certainly a baby won't be woken by his sibling crying. One of my babies was very disturbed by the organ in the church at his christening. He cried bitterly at being enclosed in unfamiliar surroundings with a terrific noise he really did not enjoy.

If your baby has been woken up by a loud noise and sounds as if he isn't going to just drop off back to sleep again then I would pick him up, wrap him snugly in a shawl and offer him a drink – a little warm milk usually makes babies sleepy. Then I would keep him on my knee for a few minutes and then gently put him down to sleep again.

Crying and illness

A baby who was not well would cry unless he was *really* ill. If he was running a temperature he would cry and whimper, and nod off a little bit, and then cry again.

His forehead and hands would feel hot and he would be listless. A baby with an ear infection which might cause a tremendous earache would cry in the night and during the day. By the time he was three months, he would rub his ear or bang his head. Earache, like many other illnesses, often first becomes troublesome at night.

You can usually tell when your child is not well because he is lethargic, flushed, cries easily, he may have diarrhoea and will have a stomach ache, or he may refuse to eat or have a high temperature. It is important for babies with high temperatures to be cooled down because of the danger of febrile convulsions. If you are at all worried, call your doctor.

One reason a new baby won't be crying

I have met people who, when their brand new baby cried, said 'Oh dear, I expect he wants his nappy changing'. Babies really and truly wouldn't care if their nappy was changed or not. Of course, they would care if they got a sore botty, but a dirty nappy doesn't worry babies – both urine and faeces are warm and comforting. People do change babies' nappies far more than they used to do. No doubt it keeps the nappy manufacturers happy.

A Quick Guide To What's Wrong - And What To Do

Little babies do get rather fussed and they begin by whimpering. When this happens during the day one needn't take much notice of it. I might walk over to him and say 'What's your problem?'

Some babies whimper in their sleep, and like little dogs they seem to be having a bad dream. But I would ignore whimpering unless it gets louder.

What to do if your baby is whimpering

Ask yourself:

1. Are the whimpers getting louder?
No? Leave him.
Yes? Gently stroke his forehead and speak quietly to him (see Some Soothing Tips page 48).

2. Has this calmed him down?
Yes? Leave him.
No? Is sun shining in his eyes or could he be too hot? If so, move him and/or give him a drink of boiled water (see Crying from being too hot, page 35).

3. Is he calmer now?
Yes? Put him gently down.
No? Did you have rather a busy day? If your baby is crying on his thumb, trying to calm himself down, he may have been with a crowd of people all day and can't relax. I would leave him alone to whimper for a while, he will probably be asleep in ten minutes.

4. Is he calmer now?

Yes? Leave him to sleep.

No? Pick him up and hold him against your shoulder
as he may have a bit of wind that needs
dispelling. Talk to him quietly and rock him a
little.

5. Has he stopped whimpering or crying?

Yes? I would now put him on your knee, wrapped in
his shawl, hold him in a cosy way and just talk
quietly to him for a little while. He will slowly
drop off to sleep and you can then gently settle
him down in his crib again.

No? If he is still crying he is probably a bit hungry so
I would give him a drink of milk. After the drink
I would wait a minute in case there was a bubble
of air stuck anywhere and then I would put him
down.

6. Is he happy now he's back in his crib?

Yes? Leave him to sleep.

No? If he fusses, stroke his forehead and speak quietly
to him for a minute or two. Go back to question 4.

Crying

At this age, babies usually cry because they are hungry.
If your baby has an insistent cry which tails off and then
gets louder again, if he stops for a moment to suck his
thumb or hand, it means he is hungry. Even if you have
just fed him, you should offer him a little more milk.
Even if he had been put down quite happily after his
meal, if a baby started whimpering and slowly began
getting louder and louder and just didn't settle then you
would know the baby was hungry and needed some
more food. Often even if the baby isn't hungry, but

wakeful or distressed you will find that if nothing else settles him, a little drink of warm milk will. Offer it as a last resort as, if you are breast feeding, it will wear you out to keep feeding him.

What to do if your baby is crying

Ask yourself:

1. Has he been disturbed from his sleep?
No? Go to question 2.
Yes? Go to question 8.

2. Is he crying or whimpering?
Whimpering? (See What to do if your baby is whimpering, page 41.)
Crying? Pick him up.

3. As you picked him up did you hear a huge burp?
No? Go to question 4.
Yes? He might have been crying because he had a pain in his tummy. If you can feel he has a hard and slightly sticking out tummy he is still windy so I would gently rub his tummy (see Does he have a windy tummy?, page 28).

4. Did he stop crying when you picked him up?
No? Go to question 5.
Yes? If the crying stops the moment he is in your arms, then he has a pain that stops when his body is straightened. You may even hear a surge of wind, then you know he might have been crying because he had a pain in his tummy. Hold him upright for a few minutes and then sit him on your knee and gently rub his tummy (see Does he have a windy tummy?, page 28). See also question 6.

5. Did he search your breast for food?

No? If he is still crying now, wrap him in his shawl
and sit with him calmly, hum a lullaby (see Some
Soothing Tips page 49). Make sure he is not ill
(see Crying and illness, page 39).

Yes? He is hungry. Even if he has just been fed, give
him some more (see Crying at the end of a feed,
page 26).

6. Does he cry like this every evening between 6 and 10 p.m.?

No? If he is still crying, wrap him in his shawl and sit
with him calmly, hum a lullaby (see Some
Soothing Tips page 49). Make sure he is not ill
(see Crying and illness, page 39).

Yes? He may have colic (see Crying and colic, page
29).

7. Does he cry like this all the time?

No? If he is still crying, wrap him in his shawl and sit
quietly with him, hum a lullaby (see Some
Soothing Tips page 49). Make sure he is not ill
(see Crying and illness, page 39). He may be a
little over-stimulated and finding it difficult to
settle (see also What to do if your baby is
whimpering, question 3).

Yes? He may be allergic to dairy products or be ill. Go
and see your doctor.

8. Has he a worried, wakeful cry?

No? If he is still crying, wrap him in his shawl and sit
quietly with him, hum a lullaby (see Some
Soothing Tips, page 49). Make sure he is not ill
(see Crying and illness, page 39) or too hot (see
Crying from being too hot, page 35).

Yes? If he was disturbed in his sleep and it sounds as
though he isn't going to drop off back to sleep

without some sort of attention I would always pick him up, wrap him snugly in a shawl and offer him a little milk to make him sleepy. Then I would keep him on my knee for a few minutes and then put him down to sleep again.

9. Has he calmed down now?

No? Try going through this list again. Once you have reassured yourself that he has a full tummy and that it is not windy and nothing is hurting him and he is not ill, then if you are feeling frustrated you will just have to leave him for ten minutes to cry whilst you try and unwind.

Yes? Go to questions 5 and 6, What to do if your baby is whimpering, or put him back in his cot.

Screaming

Crying and screaming are very different. Screaming is a very strong desperate noise from the very pit of the tummy. You can tell something is really wrong as your baby will scream as hard as he can.

What to do if your baby is screaming and screaming

Ask yourself:

1. Is your baby screaming and screaming so he keeps catching his breath?
No? Go to What to do if your baby is crying, page 43.
Yes? Pick him up straight away.

2. Is anything painful sticking into him?
No? Make quite sure there isn't a nappy pin, or something in the mattress or chair or carpet, or a

spiky thing from a clothes tag sticking into him.
See if his clothes are too tight round the middle
or round the neck.

Yes? Remove it.

3. Is he too hot or too cold?

No? Go to question 4.

Yes? If he is hot, remove some of his clothes and give
him a little drink of cold boiled water or, if he is
cold, put a hat on his head and another layer of
clothes on him (see Crying due to extreme
temperatures, page 35).

4. When you picked him up did he search your chest for food?

No? Go to question 5.

Yes? He is hungry and will only stop crying once your
nipple or a teat is in his mouth.

5. Did he stop screaming when you picked him up?

No? He is either desperately hungry (go to question 4)
or there is something wrong with him (go to
question 7).

Yes? He is either windy or ill (go to questions 6 and 7).

6. Does he have a hard tummy and/or a bluish tinge around his lips?

No? He may have a very painful sore throat or some
other illness that only a doctor can recognise (Go
to question 7).

Yes? He is windy (see question 4 in What to do if
your baby is crying, page 43).Go to question 8.

7. Is his scream unusual?

No? Go back to question 2, and work down the chart.

Yes? He might have picked up an infection or has a stomach ache. With any unusual cry I would call the doctor.

8. Does he scream like this every day?

No? Go back to question 2, and work down the chart.

Yes? If he screams every evening then he may have colic (see Crying and colic, page 29). If he screams all day as well as all night he might be allergic to dairy products, go and see your doctor about it.

9. Has he calmed down now?

No? Go back to question 2, and work down the chart. Once you have reassured yourself that he has a full tummy and that it is not windy and nothing is hurting him and he is not ill, then if you are feeling frustrated you will just have to leave him for ten minutes to cry whilst you try and unwind.

Yes? Go to questions 5 and 6, What to do if your baby is whimpering, page 41 or put him down in his cot.

Some Soothing Tips

It is almost impossible to remain calm if your child is crying and nothing makes him settle. You get more and more tense and, of course, he can tell. Often the best thing to do is to take 'time out' from the crying and go into the next room to unwind, then go back and try again, using one of the techniques described below.

*W*hen you have a restless baby and you stroke his forehead to soothe him, you must do it slowly and calmly. I always start very slowly and then see gradually if I can do it slower still. Stroking a baby's forehead does help very much to calm the fretful baby but you have to strive to be very calm and unhurried yourself no matter how difficult it may be.

1. Listen carefully to your baby's breathing, then match your own rate of breathing as nearly as possible to his. The baby will breathe much faster than your normal rate but when you have succeeded in synchronising your breathing to his, you will have achieved a rhythm.
2. Keeping your rhythm, slow it down, slower and slower, while stroking the baby's head slower and slower...
3. When you find he is well and truly fast asleep, stop stroking and, if he is in your arms, put him gently down.

By then you will be almost fast asleep yourself, but don't be tempted to sleep with him on your lap or you'll build up a situation where the baby will always want to be asleep with you.

Here are some other suggestions of ways in which you can calm yourself and your children which I have found to be helpful.

Singing lullabies

A wakeful baby or child, especially if you have got him in your arms, is often soothed if one sings or hums quietly to him. One of my children used to say 'Sing a la-la song' as I used to sing to him in a 'la, la, la' way because I can't really sing. Once my children got older I used to sing lullabies and put in my own words, usually a story about what we had done that day.

Of course singing may not always soothe a crying baby because he may be hungry, but if it is just because he is feeling miserable with a head cold or is so tired he can't go to sleep, then it might be worth trying a lullaby or two.

Playing a muscial box

Instead of singing, for one of my babies I bought a musical box to fix on to the cot which played Brahms 'Lullaby'. As I left the room I pulled the string and it played. It's very soothing, but in no time at all the child doesn't hear the music, it becomes just a comforting routine. If you forget to pull the string he indicates you should do so.

Rocking, or pushing in the pram

Putting a baby in the pram and rocking him gently, or pushing him round the park – or even just in the garden – often quietens a crying baby and sends him to sleep. Rocking seems to please babies, as was recognised in centuries past by cradles being designed for the purpose.

I would not rock a baby who wasn't crying, or a crying baby of more than four months, as he would get rather used to it which is tiresome if you are a busy person.

Movement and music

I know someone who plays Schubert to her children in the car on long journeys and they stop quarrelling and fall asleep, so it might be worth trying.

CHAPTER FOUR

When Your Baby Cries

(3 – 9 Months)

B Y NOW YOU WILL KNOW ROUGHLY WHAT YOUR BABY'S cries indicate and his crying should be getting much less. You are getting used to your baby and will have an idea of how much he likes to eat and drink and how he likes to sleep and if you stick to the things he likes this makes for a great sense of security. Babies do not like things to be different and at this age are becoming much more observant of change than a younger baby. They do notice anything at all different and some of them do mind very, very much.

Why Might Your Baby Cry Now?

At this age babies develop an affection for a certain toy, a teddy or bunny or very often something like the hem of a nightie or a piece of blanket and seem to find it very reassuring. The most useful comforter is the baby's thumb because it is always available, but often a baby will pick on some other object which then becomes indispensable and has to be taken when going on journeys. You mustn't leave it behind because the child will be desperately unhappy without his 'security blanket' or toy. I would never introduce a comforter, such as a dummy, as it may cause problems later. The child will usually find his own comforter from amongst his clothes, blankets, toys and fingers.

I once heard from a mother whose six-month-old son cried as if it was the end of the world, several times a night, each time he lost his dummy. She described herself as a 'jack-in-the-box' putting it back in again whenever he lost it.

I have never used a dummy myself but I can understand how parents are driven by their sleepless nights to introduce one to their crying child. The mother who asked me this question had herself had many interrupted nights, a situation which the dummy had gone some way towards resolving. However now the dummy had turned into a problem. I suggested she attach it to the yoke of her son's nightie, or the front of his babygrow, using a piece of ribbon and a safety pin. He would probably not be able to reach it at first but would soon find out where it was. Until then there was no other solution.

Becoming aware of changes

At this age babies are beginning to be attached to whoever is looking after them and on the whole are very reluctant to be handed over to other people. Of course, some babies will go with anybody, but on the whole babies are not really sociable at this time. There may even be some people they don't like – they don't like a person's face, or something about them and the sight of that particular person may make them cry. They may also cry if somebody they didn't know collected them or you left them with somebody strange, especially if they woke up in an unfamilar environment, or in their own house with a strange person. As children get towards nine months they are sometimes frightened by some particular thing, a noise or a dog bounding towards them. They do begin to notice so much more.

Feeling a sad atmosphere

By the time a child is nine months he understands much of what you say. He can't answer but you can see he understands by the reaction on his face. He won't yet be able to talk although he will be making 'ah' sounds, so he will still cry when he needs something, but unless he is ill the crying should be much less. If you have a baby that normally is fairly amenable and he takes to crying a lot yet doesn't seem to be developing an illness such as chicken pox, then the only thing to do is to see the doctor if the crying keeps on and on. He would probably be able to find the reason.

Another thing that may make a baby cry is a sadness in the family so, if you are worrying about something, do try to resolve it. Children do feel an unhappy atmosphere – not all children, of course, but the sensitive child. The thing is to try and have as calm a life as possible. The child doesn't need to be continually entertained, or talked to, you should just aim for a quiet time. It won't cure the crying entirely but in a way it will comfort the child who can't help having this personality and will be happier with a peaceful atmosphere. Often babies like this need a little reassurance (see pages 16-17).

When it's all too much

An over-stimulated child is really quite a common problem today. My children were brought up very peacefully with plenty of time alone in their large, wooden playpen. Playpens are out of vogue at the moment but I always put my children into them and if they were tired they would just sleep there.

Of course, a mother's life duties are different from a nanny's. Babies accept most situations but a baby who is taken about shopping, accompanying an older child to school and so on is more likely to be over-stimulated than one who is brought up largely in a nursery. Even with all these things for the mother to do I think, if she can make the time, it would be helpful to both her and the baby if she sat down after lunch, beside the baby who will be playing with his toys in the playpen, and read and relax for a short time. For the baby, it would provide a quiet time with his mother that he really would appreciate.

An over-stimulated baby is an over-tired baby who behaves as if he were fed up with everything. Offered a toy he hurls it away and cries very easily. Not a happy baby. He will fall asleep exhausted but will wake up fairly quickly after that and start to cry and have to be reassured. (See Chapters Two and Three).

Crying and feeding

At this age babies will still cry when they are hungry and if you are weaning them and have not yet established an eating pattern they may well be hungry. There will be a great deal of feeding changes in the next six months and by the end of the period your baby will no longer be only having breast or bottle feeds, but will now be eating solid foods and drinking from a cup. Take all these changes slowly (see the third Golden Rule, page 20). You may also find useful another book I wrote for the series, *Easy Weaning & First Feeding*.

Crying on changing from breast to bottle

When the time comes that you want to start transferring a baby from the breast on to the bottle you must do this gradually. It is useful if someone else, a friend or relation, offers the baby his first bottle, because if you pick him up and offer him a bottle he will be very distressed that he is not having the breast because he has always had it and can smell your milk and may not accept the bottle. I think the kindest thing is to stagger it – take a month or so over the change, not just one day all breast and the next day all bottle. I have known babies who couldn't accept the bottle. A rubber teat is quite different from a nipple and they cried and cried. Although these days teats do look very much like nipples, they are of course not as soft and taste different. Make sure that the hole is big enough so that the milk can drip into his mouth and then, if he is hungry, even though the milk too will taste different, he may take one or two tentative sucks and then he may give up because he is not having what he is used to. If some breast milk can be expressed into the bottle it might well help this transitional period because even though he won't like the strange teat when the milk drops into his mouth he will be more likely to suck it and enjoy it.

Crying when being fed solids

If a baby cries when he is being fed with a spoon it doesn't always mean he doesn't like the food. It may be because he is very hungry and instead of sucking, he has to feed from the spoon which is being continually taken in and out of his mouth. I've seen so many babies longing for the next spoonful and the person feeding them is chatting to a friend – they are like little birds with their mouths open, hoping and hoping for the next spoonful and sometimes even crying, worried in case there is no more food. Watch him carefully, let him dictate the pace at which you put the food in and you will avoid the tears.

You do have to feed babies carefully with a spoon. I always used a small metal teaspoon rather than one of those chunky plastic spoons, but metal spoons can sometimes catch the gum or the baby may bite the spoon. Sometimes the spoon seems to hurt him or he may be growing teeth and it just hits a tender spot. It is fairly momentary – you just take the spoon away and soothe him for a minute.

Crying because the food was too hot

A baby might also cry if his food was too hot. With conventional heating the first mouthful of food would probably be the hottest but I have been told that with a microwave sometimes there are hot areas so the baby might have been eating quite happily and then suddenly cry coming across a bit that was too hot. I believe if you stir microwaved food and then leave it to rest for a minute it will make it a uniform temperature throughout. I would always try the baby's food to test the temperature before giving it to him.

Sometimes babies take against their food and cry even before you give them any. This might happen because the food you gave them last time on a spoon was a little too hot, and so when you started to use a spoon next time they would remember and wouldn't want to use the spoon again. So I would very cautiously put the spoon on their lips so they can see that it is not too hot.

Crying because of the taste

Babies do on the whole prefer the pudding course. They usually like the first course but they actually enjoy the pudding course. If they are fussing about the first course I would take a spoonful of the pudding and alternate the two courses from then on. I have sometimes even given them the pudding first and when it is all eaten up then I have given them the other and they haven't then minded it. Once the pudding is finished they seem to know that now their meal is over and there is no point in fussing. If they can see it sitting there whilst they have to eat their first course they can't see why they are not having it. Or I would hide the pudding until all the first course is finished.

Crying after a feed
When you start solid food it is a whole new field for you and the baby and you really can be guided by him. Some babies eat a lot, some not very much and certainly some of them are suspicious and make a bit of a fuss which usually doesn't last very long, some cry at the end of the feed, either because they are still hungry, or because something pleasurable has stopped and they wouldn't mind it going on even if they weren't hungry.

If your child is crying for a long time after his feed - almost up until the next feed, it could be that he is hungry. Often when babies start solids they do seem suddenly to develop an enormous appetite. You start giving them a little and very quickly it is not enough and they may well cry and cry for more.

I know a mother whose child cried ceaselessly all day when he started solids, having never really cried much before. She thought he might be allergic to the food, but I suggested that he was just really hungry, having discovered an appetite. Once she gave him larger helpings he was fine.

Crying and sleeping

I always found that one of the secrets to a peaceful bedtime was a long, leisurely bath. There's nothing like water for calming children down so if they have a warm bath and it takes a bit longer than usual then they really and truly do enjoy it. Water is very soothing, one knows oneself – lying a bit longer in the bath one does relax. An early bedtime is also advisable, the same time every night, before the child gets too tired.

Crying because unable to sleep

Sometimes babies cry when they are over-tired and they need to lie down and go to sleep, but they often can't sleep simply because they are over-tired. When the baby is in bed and still can't sleep I stroke his head and just talk gently to him for a few minutes before leaving him and then quite often he has to have a good old cry before he goes to sleep. I do know of several babies who did the same. They had full tummies, no more wind, were quite comfortable but had to have a good old shout for five or ten minutes before sleeping. I don't mind leaving a baby to cry for up to ten minutes, but no longer. He can't get out of his cot and life has to go on, but after ten minutes I would see how he was (even if he had stopped crying) and if he was still crying I would calm him down. Once a child had stopped I always went to have a look to see if he was all right. Sometimes when children see you coming back into the room they start again. Of course, if he can't get to sleep I don't rush away unless I have to. I would stay, but not take the baby out of his crib, just stroke his head gently until he had fallen asleep or was getting drowsy (see Some Soothing Tips, page 48).

If you have a baby that doesn't settle and during the previous three months you took him out of his cot and brought him to where you were working or your husband cuddled him whilst you were making the dinner then now you have to try and avoid doing this because very soon it becomes a routine, something the baby expects. The later you have left it, the more difficult it will be to stop (see Chapter Two).

Crying in the middle of the night

Sometimes babies cry in the night because they are cold. They have wriggled out of their cosy coverings and they cannot wriggle back and are quite happy until 3 or 4 a.m. when the outside temperature drops. They begin to feel cold and perhaps a little insecure, and when you tuck them back into their covers they stop crying. I think most children do like being snuggled up, although a great many don't and immediately kick their covers off. Babies wouldn't have survived if they minded so terribly about being cold or tucked in. But on the whole a wakeful baby is usually either an over-stimulated or a hungry baby. If they wake repeatedly and you've given them a breast or bottle-feed when they first woke, then it probably isn't hunger.

I have had many parents contact me in despair about how little their baby sleeps. One mother got in touch with me because her six-month-old daughter slept very little during the day, only for 15-30 minutes and then she woke up. Even to get this amount of sleep her mother had to walk around with her or rock her to sleep in her pram. At night, too, she was just as unsettled and continually woke up – her mother was too tired to put her back in her cot and from six weeks had taken her into her own bed so they could all get some sleep. Sometimes she offered her a bottle but she still woke up again and again. She had been an unsettled baby ever since she was born, but in all other aspects was healthy.

I felt very sorry for this mother. I suggested that the baby did however need a different day-time routine and a different strategy at night. During the day I said that they should aim for as quiet an atmosphere as possible – at this age a baby would like a squeaky rubber toy, a little rattle and a wooden spoon or something to bang with, not a great deal of toys.

At six months a baby needs a couple of hours sleep in the daytime. So I told the mother to put her baby down in her cot to sleep during the day. She could have her 'cuddly' but she didn't need toys strung across the cot or a cot bumper. She should have the curtains left open so she was able to see everything that went on. She might be very angry at not being rocked to sleep or she might breathe a huge sigh of relief that she was being left in peace.

If she was angry I suggested that she be left for ten minutes. If she was not asleep by then I told her mother to avoid lifting her out of the cot but try stroking her head and talking gently to her. If this didn't work then she would have to pick her up, calm her down and offer her a drink of boiled water, she couldn't be left screaming. Once she had calmed down then she should be rocked to sleep as usual and then try the cot agian the next day.

At bed-time the child should be put in her cot and the curtains left undrawn so that there would be light from the street lamps and the moon, making a night light unnecessary. When she woke in the middle of the night I told the mother not to turn the light on, but to take her daughter calmly from her cot, change her nappy and, give her a small drink of milk from a cup. She should then tuck her down, stroke her face, make reassuring noises, but resist rocking her to sleep or taking her into her bed. I told the mother to be prepared for her baby to shout and advised her to leave her for ten minutes before going back.

If she had to return she should bring the child into her bed again, but she would have to try again the next night until the child got used to it and didn't cry on being put back to bed. In time her daughter would accept it when her mother put her back into the cot after changing her nappy and said 'I'm sorry, but this is where you sleep and that is where Daddy and I sleep. In the morning I'll come and fetch you for a cuddle, but you must go to sleep in your own cot.'

Crying from a nightmare
If a child's life flows peacefully and he has a feeling of well-being why should he get bad dreams? When do events start to make any impression on us? Do you still have impressions from being in the womb? If you have to be delivered by forceps is that in your mind? An extremely sensitive child may well have many impressions that will cause troubled sleep.

Very occasionally a child of this age may have a nightmare. You don't know quite what is going on but I have had a child I thought was awake and he was a little distressed and sobbing and his eyes were closed so I didn't know if he was still asleep and having the dream or on the verge of waking. If I think a child is having a bad dream I stroke the baby's shoulder and say 'Sssshhh. . .' and they just go back into an ordinary sleep.

Crying when waking
At this age when they wake up from a sleep babies might do a bit of whimpering or they might cry and cry. I would pick them up and sit quietly with them on my knee and if they had a very wet nappy I would change it and then, once they were calm I would feed them.

Crying when worried
Babies left alone for a long time, as they approach six months, do get a little fretful. Before this a baby who

has been left alone will just go to sleep but once he is older than six months he may get a lonely feeling from time to time. Although babies enjoy looking round and observing things like the leaves moving or a mobile and they enjoy lifting themselves up, they will get a little worried, if left too long alone.

Crying at bathtime

On the whole babies of this age enjoy being bathed, but occasionally one meets a child who does not enjoy it. He may have slipped out of someone's hands for a moment and be worried he might slip again. One of my children once inadvertently pushed his face into the water (not when I was bathing him I hasten to add) and for over a week, I couldn't put him into the bath, he was terrified. In the end I put his older sibling in first and then tried to put him in very, very carefully and he must have been reassured. Babies can have frightening experiences in the bath and if they don't want to go into it I would not bath them until they had got over their fear.

A mother once contacted me about her four-and-a-half-month-old son who used to love his bath, but had recently started to hate it. She thought that he was occasionally frightened by something in the bathroom, but she could not think what, and he would stop crying as soon as she smiled at him. But since the week before her son had cried furiously as soon as he was put in the water and sometimes right through to his feed.

He sounded to me to be rather young to have been minding shadows in the bathroom or anything like that. I wondered why he had suddenly become so unhappy about his bathtime and suggested that perhaps one evening the water was a little too warm or not warm enough. I told her to stop bathing him and wash him all over in a leisurely fashion and after two weeks to carefully introduce him to the bath again. I told her to always run a bath with cold water first and then warm it up and that she should test that the water temperature was just pleasantly warm by dipping her elbow into the bath. On hearing this, she realised that she had indeed been making the bath too hot for her son.

Disturbed by noise

Once they reach three months and for a few months ahead, some babies are alarmed by very loud noises – banging of doors, cars back-firing, sirens on fire engines and police cars – anything like that. They are disturbed and possibly alarmed by the noise and may burst into tears, but very soon get used to it. Some babies mind much more than others. I've seen babies when there has been a very loud bang and they've jumped and then sobbed and sobbed and other babies who don't seem to be worried at all. Once they get older the police car siren is one of the first sounds they make – not 'Dada' and 'Mama' but 'EeeAww'.

If a baby is startled by a very loud noise I would pick him up, comfort him and put him on my knee, then back down again in his cot, or wherever once he had stopped being upset.

Meeting strangers

Some children are much more amenable to meeting lots of different people and some children don't like it at all. One never knows quite why. One of my little girls took an instant dislike to an aunt who was a very nice aunt, but she was very tall and always dressed in black; something about her obviously worried this little girl.

It sometimes happens very early. You have a newish baby and the sight of an aunt or a grandmother might worry the child and make them cry. I knew a little boy who cried when he saw most of his relations. It depends on the child's personality. I am always conscious of the fact that children are really happier with the people they know well so when my children were small I never passed them round among strangers. I held the baby so they could look at him, but I didn't let them hold him just in case he would rather not be held by a strange person because very often that is the start of a little problem.

I was once consulted by parents of a six-month-old girl who since she was ten weeks had screamed if anyone (even her grand parents) so much as looked at her. The only people she would allow to hold or feed her were her parents. The mother had recently had to go back to work (for financial reasons) and the daughter was at a private nursery and was, needless to say, taking time to settle. The mother wanted to know how she could reassure her.

It is rare that a child so young cries with strangers. I said that unfortunately it would be impossible to reassure her daughter, as she was only six months, unless the mother stayed with the child which she sadly could not do and that only time would stop the little girl crying. I suggested that if the grandmother could look after her instead (or even a child-minder) that would be much better, but it would have to be a long-term commitment on the carer's part so that the little girl could feel secure. As she was a sensitive child I felt sure she would rather be with one new person than with a large group of strangers. You can't change a child's personality but you can try to help and make them feel secure.

Leaving your child

No matter how devoted a parent you are, at some time you are going to have to leave your child with someone other than yourself or your spouse. If it can be someone that the child knows well that is obviously the best thing. Otherwise it should be someone that you know well and can trust implicitly so that you can be sure that the child will be quite safe (see page 74). He will almost certainly have been very happy while you were away but on your return will probably cry because at the time he hadn't really taken it in that you were away. If the person you have left your child with is someone you know, or someone highly recommended, you know that the crying does not indicate that he has been unhappy in your absence, nor does it mean you can't leave him again.

It's best to just slip out

Children always seem to cry or fuss when their mothers return. So when you leave your child don't make a great thing of saying 'Goodbye' and 'Mummy won't be long'. If the child understands, then it will distress him that you are going. He won't be able to imagine what 'coming back' means. If you say you are going you certainly won't be able to go without the child because he is already feeling insecure. So, if it is something you have really got to do, I would make sure he is happily playing with the new person and then just slip out. Try not to leave him for longer than an hour the first time he is with someone new (See also Leaving your child, Chapters 5, 6 and 7).

Crying and illness

Where a child is cooking up an illness or developing a sore throat, there is nothing to see, but each time he swallows something it will hurt, so he might well cry. You can usually tell if a child has earache as he will keep putting his hand on the offending ear (see also Crying and illness, page 39).

One reason your baby won't be crying
When babies are growing teeth, this is a perfectly normal phenomenon. Anything nearby they grab and almost chew (and that might include your finger) as they feel they want to help and get the tooth through. They also dribble a lot, almost as if the saliva is lubricating the bit where the tooth is coming through. Quite often you have to put a towelling bib on the baby as so much saliva runs out. But I don't subscribe to the idea that any pain is caused by teething – certainly not until the molars arrive, if then. People say 'He's teething', if a baby seems off colour, or is just grizzling. I don't think babies get bronchitis, diarrhoea or earache because they are teething although this is often blamed on them. Parents should be aware of the fact that a baby up to two years will be crying for a reason other than teething and, if they can't account for it, should seek a doctor's advice. The child may have a temperature because he has an infection, not because he is teething. So if your baby is unhappy you musn't simply assume it is because he is growing teeth because it could be something quite serious. People are advised to buy little tubes of jelly to rub on the gums but this is totally unnecessary. I've watched ten children grow full sets of teeth without any trouble whatsoever excepting a hot red patch on the cheek when the molars are coming through, which may be a bit sore but shouldn't cause tears. The one time growing teeth may be a little sensitive is at meal-times (see Crying when being fed solids, page 54).

CHAPTER FIVE

When Your Baby Cries

(9 Months to 2 Years)

C HILDREN AT THIS AGE NEED SLEEP ALMOST MORE than food. Until they are two children should sleep for about an hour in the morning and roughly twelve hours at night. You can blame lack of sleep on crying and on restless, disturbed nights (although these could also be due to the onset of an infection). An over tired child may drop off to sleep at once, but not sleep for very long.

Why Might Your Baby Cry Now?

At this age children begin to cry for a variety of reasons connected with noticing changes. A child will notice mother isn't there, but won't be able to understand why, for example, that she has gone into hospital and will be home soon. He will notice that he is sleeping in a different room, but won't be able to understand that he is on holiday and will be going home soon. A child can see that someone is holding his toy but won't be able to understand that it is just being borrowed and will be returned soon. Perhaps the child's cry is a cry for help; he is hoping that if he cries then someone will get his toy back for him. Sometimes I have seen a small child who has taken another's toy handing it back once the owner has cried. Children of this age do seem to understand each other.

Growing pains

Noticing changes without understanding them can be worrying for a child, which is why children at this stage need a secure, peaceful life. Children of all ages often cry more when they are growing rapidly. It suddenly occurs to you, as you look at your child, that he's more tired and cries very easily yet he's not ill, he hasn't had a late night and you realise it is a growth spurt and he needs an extra sympathetic approach.

Crying for no reason

A child at this stage is developing all the time – he can lean forward and grasp things, he can turn over, he can sit up, and part of his development is experimenting with his voice. He's not crying, he's not distressed, he's just doing something. Sometimes children even scream with a faint sort of smile. Eventually they'll be talking, this is something they can do *now*.

A mother once asked me what she should do about her ten-month-old son who had recently started screaming at the top of his voice for no apparent reason. She thought he might be teething, but I told her it had nothing to do with this. Babies at this age do sometimes do this. Obviously you will know he is not ill because of his general behaviour and it is as if he was experimenting. It is almost as though he has discovered how to do it and so he keeps on doing it. The best thing is to ignore it which can be difficult in a crowded situation, or distract him by offering him something. Quite a lot of children do this. I have seen people saying 'Stop it!' and you can't blame them, but he isn't harming anybody so if you can ignore it, do. It is almost as if babies are screaming for joy, they clench their little hands, but I don't think it is screaming for joy. It is just something they can do and so they do it.

Crying and feeding

If you have introduced all changes slowly there should be no problems with the baby's feeding. He may still cry from hunger at the end of a meal, but he will soon be able to ask for more. He might also be crying because he doesn't want to eat any more and doesn't know how to tell you. If he changes his mind about a certain food he has liked in the past and cries when you try and give it to him, then don't give it to him. Before long he will enjoy it again.

Crying when changing from breast or bottle to cup
By nine months a child has very often stopped having a breast or bottle. If not, moving from breast or bottle on to a cup at nine months is very often a traumatic experience, especially if a child has not been introduced to a cup at an earlier stage so he is used to it. Sucking is a form of comfort and if a child has to give up this sucking suddenly they do miss it most terribly, so of course, you do have to approach the whole thing with care and do it gradually.

I have met people who have not taken time in substituting a cup for the breast or bottle and have done it in one fell swoop. The child is distraught and it really is a very unkind thing to do; he can quench his thirst from the cup but he doesn't have the pleasure and comfort of sucking. So I would also start weaning a child from the breast or bottle so the weaning process is completed by the time the baby is nine months or it will be more upsetting for him.

Crying when eating solids
At this age if a child cries in the middle of a meal the most usual reason is similar to that described in Chapter Four, page 54, either that the food he is being offered at the moment is too hot and and hurts him, or that he is afraid it might be going to hurt because he associates the food, spoon and bowl with being hurt on a previous occasion. It is difficult to get the child's confidence back. I would get another little spoon and take some and eat it myself and say 'Oooh, it's delicious – you have some'. I think you could soon overcome his fear and persuade him that it was all right.

Another reason a baby might cry in the middle of his meal is if he bites his tongue or his cheek. This does happen and it does upset the child. If that happens I always give the child a little drink and a cuddle. They might also eat some 'finger food' that is hard or particularly sharp which might make them cry out and could put them off certain food of this type for a little while .

Crying and sleeping
To my mind the main reason that children wake up in the night is that they are put to bed too late and are over-tired. I've heard mothers say 'He sleeps eleven hours, just a different eleven to your routine. I put him to bed at 8.30 and he sleeps until 7.30 in the morning. If I put him to bed at 6.30, then he would wake up at 5.30 and I would hate that'. Of course, so would I, but none of mine woke until 6.30, and even then I never took

them out of bed when they woke. I would give them a drink (until they were old enough to take the drink for themselves) and they would play gently on their own with toys or books I had left at the bottom of their bed before I went to bed. They would play for an hour when they woke. It was what they were used to. Sometimes they even fell asleep again.

Early to bed...

It also means that a child who goes to sleep at 6.30 p.m. has two more hours sleep before midnight, which may be an old wives tale but certainly leaves children much calmer. I think also that a child who goes to bed later probably doesn't sleep quite as long, though again I can't explain why, except that often children who go to bed later still wake up at much the same time as children who go to bed earlier – maybe their body clock wakes them up at sunrise or thereabouts. It's like when, as an adult, you have a patch of going to bed early and waking up early you find you do feel much better.

Crying in the middle of the night

When babies and small children cry in the middle of the night, not just a one-off, but fairly often, it really is a very difficult problem to cope with – everybody wants to sleep in the night and here is this small person who is wakeful. As with younger babies (See Crying in the middle of the night, page 58) wakefulness at night may be due to whatever has been happening during the day going round and round in their mind and so they can't relax, which means they can't have a restful sleep. Try and have a quieter time for at least a few weeks and see if that helps (see Chapter 7).

Having a fling

Sometimes children do wake in the night feeling very, very hungry. If this happens regularly, give them a larger tea at tea-time. Children might also cry in the night because they are cold, having flung off their covers and being unable to pull them back on again. I would put a child in a sleep bag or suit, but if they hadn't met one before they might not really like it very much. You could arrange for your heating to come on in the child's room (or get a timer put on a convector heater so it comes on) around 3 a.m. as the outside temperature drops. This phase won't last long as soon they will able to pull their blankets back on and snuggle down.

Comforting a crying baby at night

If a child of this age does wake up in the night I would go in straight away to find out what was wrong. If they were only half awake I would just say 'Sssshhh' and very gently stroke them and stay a little while by them. But if they were very wide awake I would take them on my knee and comfort them and then I would try and put them back in their cot after a few minutes. If there was great resistance, I would say 'Sssshhh, I'll just go and get you a nice, warm drink'. Children do understand quite a lot so they will probably be quiet and stay happily in bed while you get it. Don't worry that you are going to be getting them warm milk every night until they are 21, it is just a phase that some children go through.

Let him take his time

If a child is used to being offered milk on wakeful nights you may not even have to give him that first cuddle, but just tell him you are going to get his milk once he has started crying. When you come back I would sit him on your knee to drink it in the cosy darkness. It is essential not to hurry, to make him feel safe and that you have enough time to stay with him (though you'd much rather not). I wouldn't offer him a drink each time he woke. If he woke again I would go in but I would not take him out of the cot, but try just tucking him down.

I have had many people contact me with sleeping problems. A typical mother with a son who was almost two came to me once in despair. She had tried everything – aromatherapy, two different homoeopathic remedies, sleeping drugs, putting him to bed at different times, leaving him to cry and taking him to a sleep clinic at her local hospital. He still woke up screaming every night and would then stay awake for hours in the middle of every night. The only way she could get him to sleep was in her bed.

Sleep problems are always difficult because unless you are on the spot you can't know exactly what goes on in the household. I wondered what had triggered off the screaming, but it was impossible to find out.

I suggested that no one should talk about his problem in front of her son. I said that she would need patience (as the situation would probably not change for at least three months) and consistency – make his day as peaceful as possible and keep to the same routine every night. Her son would have been aware of all the different things she had tried on him and probably would already be wondering what was going to happen that night – which would not make for a very reassuring atmosphere. I said she should give him a bath at 6 p.m., no later or he would be over-tired, and cosily read him a story while he is lying in bed and then tuck him down to sleep. If he didn't want her to leave the room she should stay there quietly tidying up and gradually slip out.

When he cried in the night I said she should go in immediately and not turn the light on in his room; the light from the landing would be all that was needed. She should try and soothe him and bring him a drink of water if he needed one. I told her I would sit by his cot for a few minutes, holding his hand and if he was getting sleepy but not dropping off I would say 'I think I'll just go to have a little sleep in my bed. You have a little sleep in your bed and don't shout or you'll wake everyone up. I'll see you in the morning.' I added that if he did shout then she must go back in as children don't shout for the sake of it, there is a reason.

Finally, I suggested that if she had tried this for three months and it hadn't worked, and the child still wanted to come into her bed, then I would bring him in and carry him back once he was asleep. Or she could try to let him go to bed in her bed and then once she was going to bed, when the child would be really fast asleep, to try and put him into his own cot or bed. If one could do this very gently with luck he would not wake up. Going to sleep in Mummy's bed could give the child a reassuring feeling.

Crying when worried

I would not discuss with a child of this age that I was going to be out or tell him who I was going to leave him with. He still can't understand what 'going' and 'coming back' means. It is something beyond a child's comprehension because children of this age live absolutely in the present.

Leaving your child
You will worry a little, especially the first time you leave a child, but you must try very hard not to let him know that you are worried. His life should carry on just

as it would have done if you were there sitting on the floor playing with him in surroundings he knows. Very often children of this age are happier if they are not taken out on a little walk by a new person, they are much happier on their home territory. The 'babysitter' must achieve a rapport with the child before you leave, so once you notice this is happening, just slip in and out of the room a few times so the child is used to you coming and going, and when you do go they will know you are coming back. You've gone out of the room and they won't even think about it while you aren't there, but they will cry on your return. All children do at first, no matter how happy they have been with the babysitter.

Find someone you can trust

If you feel you must have someone sitting in with your baby in the evening to enable you to go out, it is really essential if you go out fairly often to have the same person always and of course initially to make absolutely sure that she is reliable. Unless she has been recommended by a close friend of yours it is most important to speak to a person who has employed her previously to make absolutely sure that it is a bona fide reference. Obviously it is best if the sitter first arrives before the baby has gone to bed so that he can see her. You don't need to do much more than introduce them. Some babies are very friendly and some babies are not so friendly but at least he will have seen the person who will be sitting downstairs and so won't get upset if he wakes up in the middle of the night – he will see a face he recognises.

Write down anything relevant the sitter needs to know about your baby – such as how you can calm him down if he wakes in the night – and leave the telephone number where you will be. Tell the sitter that if he simply won't settle she must let you know because if he cries and gets into a state he may well be very sad the next time you go out, especially if he sees the same babysitter.

Crying and illness

When children are tired or ill they become, as it were, a year younger. You will see how an ailing or exhausted child of three is like a little two-year-old and a child of two is like a one-year-old. When they are ill this is very evident, but also at bedtime when they are tired they grow a year younger and should be treated as such. Read them a story you would have read them a year ago and comfort and soothe them correspondingly.

Crying from falls

It is an interesting fact that if a child falls and you just wait for him to get up he won't cry, but if you rush forward and pick him up and cuddle him, he does cry. Of course, if he splits his knee this would make him cry, but children tumble a lot when they are learning to walk and it never makes them cry. If from the beginning when they fall you just quietly wait for them to scramble to their feet they don't cry. I've also seen children fall and cry and the mother has walked up and said 'Get up yourself!' I felt very sorry for those children. Older nannies, if a child fell very hard and banged his head or any part of his body rather badly, would make the child spend a penny. I don't know why. I wonder if the idea was that it would make them relax?

CHAPTER SIX

When Your Child Cries

(2 – 5 Years)

A TWO-YEAR-OLD WOULD CRY IF HE WAS TIRED, HE wouldn't scream but cry miserably. A child who is exhausted at this age will cry so easily, almost in frustration, he won't know why he feels so wretched.

Two-year-old children are famous for having tantrums. They are now able to do many more things but sometimes what they would like to do they are still unable to do, either because it is forbidden or because they can't yet do it themselves for a variety of reasons. This leads to outbursts of temper that are very annoying for everybody round about, so before they get to this stage try and implement a calm life for your child. Tantrums may go on until the child is five or six. If these become worrying, you may find useful another book I wrote for this series, *Coping with Temper Tantrums*.

Why Might Your Child Cry Now?

Three-year-olds mind terribly about any disappointment, they cry and stamp their feet. They also resent play being interrupted. They are often very angry when it's time for lunch and they would really rather go on playing. They will of course also cry angrily if another child snatches a toy from them. Once they get a little older they become more amenable because they understand much more.

Children of four and five are so much more conscious of what's going on around them and may cry when a holiday, or a weekend, or a tea-party has come to an end as they don't want to leave their friends, or finish the fun. Five-year-olds will cry because they want to finish a game and not break if off for bedtime, 'Can't I just finish it?'. Like younger children they will also cry with disappointment if a treat that they were looking forward to is not forthcoming.

Trouble at school
They will also cry about something happening at school like the teacher not being fair or one of the children being a bit of a bully – things that you don't know about. If they don't want to go to school I would try and find out why that is. If they are being teased or bullied they often don't tell you and if you ask them they insist that everything is all right. You must get to the bottom of it or it might possibly get worse and it would be awful if your child dreaded going to school. Always be very much on your child's side and, if necessary, have a word with the teacher about it.

If children of any age are incubating an illness of some kind they cry very easily, just whimpering, the slightest thing seems to turn on the taps. That's how you get the idea that all is not well. It may only be two days later that the cold or some infection develops and then you look back and say 'So that's why they were so unhappy the other day'. When a child is developing an illness or infection they do cry more than usual. They might also feel a little sadder after the illness, as it will have taken a lot out of them.

Crying and sleeping

Oddly enough, the more tired a child is, the less he wants to go to bed. Some cry at bedtime because they are over-tired. They should have an early bedtime just as they are beginning to feel sleepy so they can enjoy going to bed. If they always go to bed at the same time there shouldn't be any question of tears. Putting off bedtime is going to make the child more tired and therefore possibly not so happy about going to bed.

Crying from night-time fears

Any time between the ages of two and four a child may begin to have bedtime fears. They shed a year or so when they go to bed and things that wouldn't have fussed them earlier in the day loom larger in the child's imagination – perhaps a slightly frightening story they have read, an adventure story, might worry them and they imagine various creaks and bangs. Very often it is an imaginary creature that scares them but a child may simply be afraid of the dark. If a child is over-tired, things magnify at night in the same way as they do for adults who have a serious problem. There comes a time when the child says 'Leave the door open' and then, of course, I always do.

I think parents with small children would be very well advised to monitor closely what their children see on television. Disney films are not really suitable for children under the age of six. They may say 'Mummy, I'm not frightened' but subconsciously they are and they do very often have nightmares about something they have seen that can recur. In this television age I do appreciate that it is very difficult for parents with small children but I think it is far better to be playing a game or reading a story. Children needn't watch television at all – I certainly don't think there ought to be a routine of watching television every single day just because it is there.

I once heard from a mother with a two-and-a-half-year-old child who had night fears. They lived in a large Victorian house on a busy road and the mother said that at night her little boy was afraid of the noises, the rain on the window and the car doors banging.

It seemed to me that the child was quite young to have such specific fears – I think he must have overheard something an adult had remarked and the ideas must have been put into his head. I said to the mother that she should be on his side and agree with him, 'I don't like the noise either. It doesn't last very long and it doesn't actually do any harm to anybody but I don't like it and I will be jolly glad when it stops. I really don't like it.' I said it was very likely that he would be surprised to hear that his mother didn't like the noise either and would hold her hand and comfort her. The act of comforting her would stop him being afraid.

Crying in the middle of the night
I remember walking along the road with one of my children, three years old, both of us feeling like zombies after another night of her continual crying. But it didn't mean the little girl slept any better the next night. I used to so look forward to my monthly night off. I was on the floor above her and she used to come into my bed every night once she could walk. I wish I could have

shared a room with her – it might have helped. I never knew why she started crying every night in her second year but it lasted until she was six. By then she didn't cry, but came into my room and slipped into my bed for a matter of minutes and then went back to her bed and sweetly slipped the covers back over me again.

Occasionally children may wake because they have a tummy upset or an infection which results in diarrhoea, if you have a child who wakes up a lot in the night it really is a problem that is hard to cope with. You simply must go in and reassure him and perhaps offer a warm drink (See Crying in the middle of the night, page 70).

Turn his return into a treat

If you have more than one child it very often helps if the wakeful child can share a room with his siblings. Even if he cries he won't wake up the others. Or you could try bringing their cot or bed into your room so he feels secure as you are nearby.

Of course the moment will come when you want him to go back into his room, and this could be tricky, you would have to be very positive about it. Get it all organised and one day when he comes out of the bath, take him into his bedroom where his cot is already waiting. Say to the child, making it sound like a special treat, 'I've moved your cot into this room so that you and teddy can have it all to yourselves.'

If you have decided to give some strategy a try, you must give it at least a couple of weeks. See that he has the chance to do lots of running about in the fresh air – if you live near a park he can run about without any fear of traffic – or take a ball to play with. And also arrange for him to spend a happy hour or so, possibly with a child the same age, so he has an interesting day. As with so many problems in childhood, it is essential to aim for peaceful days.

A mother once asked me what she should do about her two-year-old son who woke every night and screamed. Either she or her husband went to him at once and she said it could take up to an hour to settle him. He slept for an hour in the morning and went to bed at 6.30 p.m. very happily, with his door shut and no light on. She had tried a night light but it had not helped. He had started climbing out of his cot so he now slept with the side down but she wondered if he needed to go into a bed.

I suggested that the onset of two years did often bring problems of one sort or another; as children get a little bit older a few more fears creep in. I told her that she was right to go to her little boy when he cried in the night and right to leave the side of his cot down so he could get out in the morning. I said she should try leaving the curtains open and also his door so that as he was dropping off to sleep he would feel nearer to her – feeling more secure, and might well sleep all night.

I added that when he woke in the middle of the night, rather than take an hour to settle him, I would have a mattress in his room so that I could drop off to sleep next to him. Some children just are insomniacs, so there is no reason why the person responsible should lose their sleep too. I think it is important that the parent can lie down and sleep, even if the child can't.

Crying from a nightmare

Once a child is two you will know if he has had a bad dream. He may say something like 'Big dog, big dog!' which gives you a clue. Most children do go through a period of bad dreams. Even after a very happy day they may have a nightmare and you don't really know why – you might have been out with the child and he saw a very big dog. The child wakes up and cries and may or may not be deeply distressed. In extreme cases when they scream, something terrifying has apparently invaded their sleep and it is best to then take them out of their cot or bed and reassure them. I would take them on my knee and then I would wake them up so they were really wide awake. I have known children open their eyes wide and look amazed that whatever has frightened them isn't there and then they have become very sleepy again and I put them back to bed. Unless they have asked for a drink I would just put them back to bed.

Comfort and reassure them

If the crying isn't severe, a child may not even open his eyes, he may be half awake, and then I just stroke his shoulder and say 'Sssshhh' and he just drifts back to sleep. Children do have recurring dreams – some particular thing has brought on a bad dream in the past and for a time it comes back again and again. You just have to reassure them when it happens.

I've had children come rushing into my bed in the middle of the night, almost as if they were being chased – all you can do is comfort them. I have then let them sleep in my bed and they may take themselves back to their own beds later, they may not. I think some children try to not go to sleep in case 'that horrible man comes'. If that were the case I would sit beside the child's bed and hold his hand until he had dropped off to sleep.

Crying when waking

Some children cry when they wake from an afternoon sleep and I still don't know why. I know when I wake from my middle of the day nap my mouth feels wrong and sometimes I do feel very much out of sorts when I first wake up. After my cup of tea I'm all right. If your child cries on waking I would give him a fruit drink or a cup of milk, whatever you know your child likes best.

Crying when worried

Some children mind being left with a 'babysitter' much, much more than others – some never turn a hair. I think it depends on who they are being left with – how well they know the person they are being left with and whether or not the person they are being left with has a sympathetic personality or not. It also depends on whether they are left very often or not – a child who is regularly left will probably be more used to it and will just accept it, whereas children who are rarely left often mind very much.

Once a child is three, and can grasp the meaning of 'going out' and 'coming back', I would tell him where I was going and who would be looking after him.

Leaving your child

Some children around this age do cry hysterically when their mother leaves to go out, or in my case, because I was the principal carer, sometimes when I left to go out. I think that a mother has her own life and if she wants to go out she must. She should ask the 'baby-sitter' to come early enough to meet the child in an unhurried way (or reacquaint herself with the child) before she goes out. If possible she should arrange the times of her outings so that they are not just at the most vulnerable moments in the child's life, such as when he is starting a new school or has just come back from a long holiday with her. If the child is ill, the mother may well choose to stay at home. An ill child may feel very sad if his mother goes out and should be treated with an extra degree of sensitivity. (See also Leaving your child, pages 64 and 73).

A mother asked me what she should do about her two-and-a-half-year-old son who often cried when she left the playroom to cook lunch, or even to go to the loo. She said that she could leave him with his father or a close friend, but that he had become increasingly clingy over the past year – ever since the nanny he had had from birth had left. Since then he had had two short-lasting replacements and also a seven-month-old baby brother. His mother had now given up work but felt as if she had acquired a little shadow.

I said that her son did sound a little insecure at present which might have something to do with all the women who had recently gone out of his life. I suggested he might think that his mother would do the same thing and so she needed to aim to make him feel secure. I advised her to take him with her wherever she went. Each time she left the room she should simply say 'Come on, sweetie, I'm going to make lunch/go to the loo. Let's go'. Quite soon he would be happy not to come with her because her comings and goings will become something that are no longer 'forbidden'. I also asked her not to talk about her son wanting to be with her to friends or family in his presence or it would exacerbate the problem. Children's feelings should be respected and just as you would never talk about an adult in their presence, so you should not talk about a child either.

Crying at parties

Strangely enough, children sometimes cry hysterically at their own birthday parties. This is mainly because they are over-stimulated with the excitement of the occasion. A lot of children in one room playing exciting games and sitting down to a delicious tea is so different from everyday life that although one would expect a child to enjoy his own birthday party, he can't because it is so overwhelming. A lot of it is the noise, a lot of it is that he might not have slept very well the night before from anticipation and has woken very early in the morning to see his presents. He is looking forward to the party and it is all very stimulating.

Don't talk too much about it

People do talk a great deal to their children about things before they happen – 'Should we have Punch and Judy?', 'I wonder what presents you'll get tomorrow?' Questions like that probably make a child slightly worried as well as excited because it sounds as if their parents aren't really in control. Our parties were always much smaller than the ones today. We had a sort of 'rule' – one little guest for every year of the child's age. It worked very well.

Sometimes guests cry and cry at parties too. In that case if I was in charge of a crying guest I would take him home or I would stay at a party if my child wanted me to and I would never force him to join in anything. Even if a child who was not my responsibility felt sad I would take them aside and reassure them, not push them into joining in. On rare occasions we have had to ask the mother to collect a sobbing guest. One of my little girls just wanted to know I was there so I used to sit quietly in another room. I wouldn't have said 'You're a big girl now, you'll be all right'. One of my girls wanted me to stay and held my hand firmly throughout the party – she's my most gregarious 'child' now, I would say.

CHAPTER SEVEN

My Tried and Tested Routines

I ALWAYS FELT THAT WITH THIS ROUTINE I KNEW WHERE I was. Of course, I couldn't always stick rigidly to it, but that didn't matter. It gave me a structure and the baby soon got used to it. Don't worry if the first six weeks of your baby's life don't seem to fit in with the routine, sooner or later he will settle down.

With a first baby you can be a bit more flexible but if there are other children the new baby's routine will have to fit in with them, especially if they are at school.

New Born Baby To Four Months

A . M .

2.00 (If the child wakes). Breast or bottle feed and nappy change. Then back into his crib.
(When they are very new babies almost always wake up with a hungry tummy. I would give him some milk, not warm boiled water or he will be awake

again in half an hour. If he does not wake I would not
wake him.)

6.00 Breast or bottle feed and nappy change. Then back
into his crib.
(I would expect him now to sleep through to 9.30 a.m.)

9.30 Bath, then nappy change and clean clothes.
(If awake. If not, I would leave him to sleep until 10 a.m.,
but no longer.)

10.00 Breast or bottle feed, then back into his pram.
(He would probably be awake and looking around
perfectly happily before going to sleep.)

11.00 Put him in the fresh air.
(If it was good weather I would put the pram outside and
the fresh air would put the baby to sleep. If the weather
was bad I would still have put him out as we had such
sturdy coach-built prams and he was snuggled down.
Without a coach-built pram I would leave him inside and
keep the windows open. If you need to go shopping or
take an elder sibling to the park then you could do it now).

P . M .

1.00 Nappy change and change of scene. Breast or bottle
feed if needed.
(If I heard him shouting I would turn him around in his
pram so he would have a change of scene or bring him
in, change his nappy and put him on the floor of the
playpen under a mobile. If he was really fed up I would
feed him a little bit earlier.)

2.00 Breast or bottle feed and nappy change.
(Unless you have fed him or changed his nappy earlier,
see above.)

2.30 Put him in his pram.
(see 11 a.m.).

4.00-4.30 Fruit juice.
(I wouldn't wake him up for his fruit juice, but babies usually do seem to be awake by now. At one month old I start to give him a little drink of very diluted fruit juice from a teaspoon. Once he is six weeks old I give it to him from a cup. After that I put him on his back in the playpen or on a rug on the floor so he could look around. I wouldn't play with him. If he is restless and grizzles it means he is hungry or tired, so I would move on to feed and bed earlier.)

5.30-6.00 Top & tail.

6.00 Breast or bottle feed. Then into his crib.
(If you can, make this a cosy time, wrapped up in a shawl, all by yourselves, with a dim light for company.)

10.00 or 11.00 Breast or bottle feed and nappy change, then back into his crib.
(Either wake him for this feed or leave him to sleep until he wakes up hungry.)

Five Months To Eight Months

For the next four months the routine remains the same with only one change each month which is to slowly introduce a baby to solids and wean him from the breast or bottle.

Five months old

10.00 a.m. Replace the breast or bottle with a cup.
(I allow weaning from the bottle and breast to take four months – I think it is unkind to do it any quicker.)

Six months old

2.00 p.m. Solid feed and replace the breast or bottle with a cup.
(At this feed I first introduce solids and replace the second breast or bottle feed with a cup.)

Two weeks later
10.00 a.m. Solid feed followed by milk from a cup.
(I now introduce baby cereal for breakfast).

One week later
6.00 p.m. Solid food feed followed by bottle or breast feed.
(I now introduce baby cereal for tea.)

Seven months old

6.00 p.m. Solid feed and replace the breast or bottle with a cup.
(I now replace the bottle or breast feed with a cup for the third feed.)

Eight months old

6.00 a.m. Replace the breast or bottle with a cup.
(Very often babies don't wake up at this time and so don't need anything until breakfast which should then be given at 8 a.m. as in the routine below.)

Nine Months To One Year

A.M.
7.00 Fruit juice and nappy change then back to bed with a few toys.
(This may be earlier or later depending on when your baby wakes up.)

8.00 Breakfast, then pot, then play
(Once a baby is nine months I put him on the pot once a day so he gets used to it. After that I put him in the playpen with a few toys until he can walk when I put the playpen away and he plays in the nursery which has a safety gate on the door.)

10.00 Put him outside in his pram.
(I put him in his pram – either sitting-up or lying down or kneeling up depending on whether he is a sitter-upper – and wrap him up well if it is winter. I give him something to play with and mostly after a while he would just curl up and go to sleep. Very often babies throw the toys out as far as they can and then go to sleep. When he wakes up I don't rush out but leave him there to sit and watch until he has had enough or it is lunch-time. This would also be a good time to take him shopping or to the park with you.)

P . M .

12.30-1.00 Lunch, then nappy change or pot, then play.
(From eleven months I would put the baby on the pot after lunch as well as after breakfast and tea – until then I would change his nappy at this time. As at 8 a.m. I would put him to play in the playpen until he could walk.)

2.00 Go to the park.
(We would go to the park for two hours unless the weather was bad when we would stay in the nursery. Once we got back I would make tea and he would play in the nursery or come out with me if I had to shop.)

4.30-5.00 Tea, then pot.
(Once the baby was ten months old I put him on the

pot after tea as well as after breakfast.)

5.00 Play.
(This was the time that the children I looked after played with their mother.)

6.00 Bathtime.

6.30 Drink of milk, then bed and story.
(Until a baby is nine months old I always feed him at 10 p.m. as I don't think it is fair that he should have his last meal at 6 p.m.. Once he is over nine months I would give him a drink of milk now if he asked for it.)

One Year To Five Years

For the next four years the routine remains more or less the same. Gradually they will be sitting on the loo rather than having to have their nappy changed, their meals will get larger and they will need less sleep. The main change in routine comes with the introduction of school.

One year old

6.30 p.m. Bed and story.
(At this age I stop giving the baby a drink of milk at bedtime because he has had a mug of milk at tea-time. If a child is thirsty at bedtime then of course I would give him a drink.)

Two years old

10 a.m. Go to the park.
(I no longer put him out in the pram, instead I take him to the park for an hour.)

11 a.m. Juice and rest.
(Once we had returned from the park he would play quietly in the nursery for an hour before lunch. On our return from the park I would give him a drink of fruit juice and then put him to bed fo an hour before lunch).

12 p.m. Lunch then rest
(After lunch I would put him in his room with a book for roughly an hour, sometimes he fell asleep and sometimes he didn't. He would be quite happy just to be on his bed. Then he would play in the nursery before we went out to the park again.)

Three years old

The routine continues as for the two year old unless your child is starting nursery school when it will need some juggling around.

Four years old

9 a.m Play (either in the garden or in the nursery).

11 a.m. Juice and reading lesson.
(With a blackboard we would do letters and numbers. I taught all my children to read when they were four.)

11.15 a.m. Park.
(We would take a ball and meet other children.)

1 p.m. Lunch then rest.
(No nap was necessary but some children get tired quicker than others. I would put him to bed with a book and sometimes he would just sleep.)

A note from Nanny

When babies cry incessantly you really and truly
wonder if it will ever, ever end. And of course it
does eventually. You really do forget how awful it
was – you remember it happening but you can
hardly recall your despair and disappointment
that the baby was being so tiresome. At the time
you were very depressed because you were tired
and because whatever you did didn't have any
effect, or very little. When the disturbed nights
end, you have a very great sense of relief; it is so
wonderful when they stop. At first you can
hardly believe that this extremely stressful period
of your life is behind you and you will almost be
waiting for it to start again and soon it is a
wonderful feeling to know that when you get
into bed you will be there until the next morning.
It really is marvellous when it is all over.

I think a baby that cries in the night is one of the
worst problems you have to cope with. Because
of this wakeful child you can't get your sleep and
so it is difficult for you to cope. Various other
childhood problems don't rest on the fact that
you can't sleep.

Unfortunately there is no magic wand that you
can wave to stop a baby crying immediately, but I
have suggested various reasons why a baby cries
and have, I hope, helped you to solve the
problem.

Good luck!

Index